RACHEL CARSON

The Environmental Movement

by
John Henricksson

New Directions
The Millbrook Press
Brookfield, Connecticut

*To the Wildwood librarians . . . and, now that I think
about it, to all librarians everywhere.*

Produced in association with Agincourt Press.
Interior Design: Tilman Reitzle
Editorial Consultant: William Hohman

Photographs courtesy of: Rachel Carson Council: 6 (Eric Hartman), 19,
22, 43 (Shirley Briggs), 49; New York Times: 8; Beinecke Rare Book and
Manuscript Library, Yale University: 16, 46, 53, 58; Chatham College: 26,
30; The Bettman Archive: 63, 72, 85, 88; AP/Wide World Photos: 81.

Selected quotations from *The House of Life: Rachel Carson at Work* by Paul
Brooks. Copyright © 1972 by Paul Brooks. Reprinted by permission of
Houghton Mifflin, Inc.
Headlines on page 8 copyright © 1962 by The New York Times
Company. Reprinted by permission.

Cataloging-in-Publication Data

Henricksson, John.
Rachel Carson: the environmental movement.

100 p.; ill.: (New directions)
Bibliography: p.
Includes index.

Summary: A biography of the biologist Rachel Carson,
focusing on the events that led her to expose pesticide
pollution in her book *Silent Spring* and her legacy as a
founder of the environmental movement.
1. Carson, Rachel, 1907-1964. 2. Air—Pollution.
3. Water—Pollution. I. Title. II. Series.
B (92)
ISBN 1-878841-16-5

Contents

Introduction 5

1 Thunderstorm 7

2 The Born Writer 17

3 Turning Point 25

4 I Must Go Down to the Seas 31

5 Triumph 41

6 The Writer's Life 52

7 Hidden Catastrophes 60

8 Noisy Summer 71

9 Choices 83

Important Events in Rachel Carson's Life 91

Notes 92

Suggested Reading 93

Index 94

Many books have been written about Rachel Carson. Three of these are: *The House of Life* by Paul Brooks, who was Carson's editor and longtime friend; *Sea and Earth* by Philip Sterling, a biography for young adults; and *Silent Spring Revisited* by Frank Graham, Jr., which examines the results of *Silent Spring*. These books were the starting point for my research. As an author I am grateful for their scholarly work. As a reader I am grateful for the hours of pleasure they have given me.

Dr. Robert Panza, Patricia Panza, and Ken Carlson of the Rachel Carson Homestead Association in Springdale, Pennsylvania, have been very helpful in providing historical and biographical information. Shirley Briggs, executive director of the Rachel Carson Council in Chevy Chase, Maryland, was Rachel Carson's close friend and coworker at the U.S. Fish and Wildlife Service for many years; she provided a wealth of personal information. Council biologist Nathan Irwin supplied much information concerning current pesticides and their use. I also want to acknowledge the valuable help of Orville and Connie Gilmore—father and daughter, English teacher and librarian—whose love of books and the natural world brought a special luster to their contribution.

John Henricksson

Introduction

As we move toward the twenty-first century, more and more people are becoming aware of the premier challenge we face, that of saving our natural world from destruction at our own hands. But this awareness of environmental issues is a recent development. Forty years ago, most people felt that scientific progress and the activities of factories had little serious impact on the environment. Rachel Carson was one of the few people who understood that pollution and the growth of cities were having a devastating effect on plants and animals, rivers and oceans—even the air around us.

When *Silent Spring*, Rachel Carson's powerful look at the horrible effects of pesticide abuse, was published in 1962, it upset many powerful people. Heads of corporations and the scientists who worked for them had made a lot of money creating the chemicals that Rachel Carson criticized. Yet despite their stiff resistance, Carson continued to champion her cause and refused to back down. Today, environmental activists have set up recycling centers, attempted to stop the construction of nuclear power plants, and participated in Earth Day activities that dramatize environmental concerns. As a result, the environmental movement has begun to make our world a cleaner, safer, more beautiful place.

We have much left to do if we hope to preserve the environment. But because of Rachel Carson's ideas and the way she put them into words, we have a better chance to succeed.

Eric Hirsch
Assistant Professor of Sociology
Providence College

*Rachel Carson was the founder of the
modern environmental movement.*

1

Thunderstorm

"Thanks to a woman named Rachel Carson, a big fuss has been stirred up to scare the American public out of its wits."[1] So began an article that appeared in the *Saturday Evening Post* in September 1963. It was one of hundreds of stories printed all across the United States, and around the world, in the year following the publication of a book called *Silent Spring.*

In fact, the "fuss" actually began before the book's publication. When *The New Yorker* printed large selections of *Silent Spring* in June 1962, months before the book was due to come out, the magazine was flooded with mail. People wrote to their representatives in Congress. Newspaper editors sent reporters out to cover the story. The *New York Times* headlined an article about the affair: " 'Silent Spring' Is Now Noisy Summer."

And the noise wasn't all amiable. "There is no doubt about the impact of *Silent Spring*," said *Time* magazine. "[I]t is a real shocker." *Time* claimed that "scientists, physicians, and other technically informed people" would see the book as "one-sided, and hysterically overemphatic."[2]

Similar reactions came from a variety of sources. Farmers were furious. College professors were outraged. Edwin Diamond, the writer of the *Saturday Evening Post* article, declared that Carson wanted to bring the planet "back to a dark age of plague and epidemic."

PESTICIDE FOUND IN JERSEY DRUGS

State Bars Distribution of Items Made in Hoboken

Special to The New York Times.

TRENTON, Aug. 30 — The New Jersey Department of Health today barred further distribution of certain drugs found to be contaminated with two insecticides.

A spokesman for the department identified the insecticides as lindane and chlordan. He said they would not necessarily cause death if taken internally by a human, but would have an adverse effect, depending on the number of pills consumed.

The health official said the contaminated drugs were all manufactured by the Kingston Laboratories of 321 Newark Street, Hoboken. Dr. Roscoe P. Kandle, State Health Commissioner, said the company had been experimenting with insecticide pills.

Lyonel Berken, president of

U. S. Sets Up Panel to Review The Side Effects of Pesticides

Controls Studied—Kennedy Finds Work Spurred by Rachel Carson Book

By MARJORIE HUNTER
Special to The New York Times.

WASHINGTON, Aug. 30—The effectiveness of Government programs dealing with the use and control of pesticides is under review by a special Federal committee.

This was disclosed today after President Kennedy's assurance at his news conference yesterday that the Government is examining its pesticide program.

The President was asked if Government agencies were taking a closer look at the possibility of dangerous, long-range side effects from the widespread use of pesticides. He replied:

"Yes. I—and I know that they already are—I think, particularly, of course, since Miss Carson's book, but they are examining the matter."

He was referring to Rachel

Rachel Carson
Brooks

ture is engaged in extensive research to find other methods of controlling and eradicating

U. S. FINDS STORES GOT THALIDOMIDE

Says Barred Drug Reached Many Pharmacy Shelves

Special to The New York Times.

WASHINGTON, Aug. 30—The Food and Drug Administration said today that a number of pharmacies in this country had stocks of thalidomide.

This was the first indication that the drug, blamed for the deformities of thousands of babies abroad, ever reached the shelves of drug stores in the United States.

Thalidomide was tested extensively on Americans but was never cleared for sale by the Food and Drug Administration.

Agency officials declined to say how the drug had reached pharmacy shelves. It might have been imported from abroad, or it could have been contributed by some of the doctors to whom the drug was sent for testing on patients.

The manufacturer, William S. Merrell Company of Cincinnati,

given authority scription files recall a "dange drug" from the asked for auth drug store files and amphetami The report w the House Com state and For The committee two drug ref passed unanim by the Senate similar one sp Administration. "The retail d torically been" tion drugs," th stated. It said that t through April, 1,100 prosecuti ??? ill... .. ..l. drugs ended in of about 1,900. "In almost 8! cases, the defe were druggist. ployes," the r "During the sa have been only against a total ical practitione The agency dozens of com them among th

Carson and pesticides made headlines in 1963.

What kind of book could bring about such intense reaction? What was at the center of the thunderstorm surrounding *Silent Spring*?

Rachel Carson, the author, was an unlikely person to stir up controversy. She was 55 years of age, an unassuming woman with a gentle, searching expression. She was a trained biologist who had worked for many years at the U.S. Bureau of Fisheries and the Fish and Wildlife Service. She had written three popular books about the sea and shore, one of which, *The Sea Around Us,* became a best-seller. She was an avid bird watcher, a cat fancier, and a lover of the outdoors.

It was this love and respect for nature that led Rachel Carson to a world of fame and controversy. Her previous books were beautifully written accounts of sea life, describing "slender shapes of sharks moving in to the kill" and "long-stalked kelps that sway in dusky forests." They contained little in the way of alarm at the ways human technology was threatening that life. These books were written in the 1940s and 1950s, at a time of prosperity in America . . . and before people fully realized the price they were paying for that prosperity.

In the years between the end of World War II in August 1945, and 1962, the United States had experienced unprecedented growth. Americans were sure that science would continue to improve their lives, and with good reason. In the four years of the country's involvement in World War II, science had created jet planes, rockets, computers, and atomic power. Americans believed that technology would continue to improve their lives during peacetime.

And they were right. Improvements were made in agriculture that made American farming the wonder of the world. Farm production became so great that the government paid farmers to take land out of production and spent $1 billion a year to store the excess food.

This explosion in farm output was due in part to the development of new machines. Tractors, threshers, harvesters, and combines made it vastly easier for farmers to till soil and plant and harvest crops.

The other "stars" of the agricultural boom were the pesticides and herbicides. Scientists working for chemical companies declared war on two of the farmer's ancient enemies: weeds and insects. Pesticides are, simply, chemicals that kill pests (the -cide suffix comes from the Latin word for killer), and herbicides kill weeds. These chemicals were easy to use and stunningly effective.

Beyond that, some pesticides actually promoted health. Typhus, malaria, and other dreaded diseases were wiped out or kept in check by pesticides that killed the carriers. To many, it seemed only a matter of time before all insect-borne diseases would be eliminated.

The American public thought well of pesticides. Because of pesticides, more people were fed with less toil, and many lives were saved. If the pesticide companies had wanted to, they could have run advertising campaigns declaring "Pesticides and You: A Perfect Match" or "Pesticides Are Your Pals." But they didn't need to. Americans already believed it.

Well, not everybody believed it. As the decades went by and more and more gallons of pesticides soaked into farmlands, some people began to wonder about the side effects of these chemicals. Evidence mounted that traces of these pesticides remained in food and poisoned humans who consumed it. Further evidence seemed to indicate that pesticides in the soil leaked into groundwater, lakes, and streams, poisoning them and the wildlife that depended on them.

Rachel Carson and her book *Silent Spring* made the American public aware of these dangers. But Rachel Carson was not America's first environmentalist. In the nineteenth century Henry David Thoreau spent two years alone in a cabin and wrote *Walden,* a book proclaiming, among other things, that humans ought to learn to protect wildlife because the balance of nature is important to human well-being. Later writers, such as John Muir, John Burroughs, Aldo Leopold, and David Brower, warned about the continued abuse of nature in the name of progress.

But these were voices lost in the excited babble about progress and technology. In 1962 most Americans had scarcely even heard the word "environment."

In that year, however, people around the world started becoming aware of the dangers of using poorly tested chemicals. In 1959, a tranquilizing drug called thalidomide had gone on sale in Europe. Over the next three years, the drug was widely sold, and many of those who used it were pregnant women. Then, in early 1962, it was discovered that thalidomide was responsible for thousands of disfiguring birth defects. Until this time, most doctors had believed that chemicals in a pregnant woman's body would not affect her unborn child.

The thalidomide horror made people around the world aware of the disastrous effects of using chemicals which had not been adequately tested. A few years before, the American public might not have taken a book about chemical dangers to the environment quite as seriously. But now people had learned a terrible lesson about the side-effects of progress. And they were prepared for others.

Rachel Carson was one of those who had been steadily amassing evidence of the harm that pesticides were causing. *Silent Spring* was a chilling warning. In it Carson wrote:

> These sprays, dusts, and aerosols are now applied almost universally to farms, gardens, forests, and homes—nonselective chemicals that have the power to kill every insect, the "good" and the "bad," to still the song of birds and the leaping of fish in the streams, to coat the leaves with a deadly film, and to linger on in soil—all this though the intended target may be only a few weeds or insects.[3]

These words had an explosive impact on the American public. It suddenly occurred to millions of people that the great economic boom they had been living in had a terrible dark side that they hadn't noticed. In this sense, *Silent Spring* was more like a horror story than a scientific book. Rachel Carson even began the book with a kind of science-fiction description of a pretty little town into which peril quietly creeps.

"There was once a town in the heart of America where all life seemed to be in harmony with its surroundings," the book begins.[4] In this town, people, trees, and animals all live peacefully. Then, slowly, a strange silence grows over the town. The birds have stopped chirping, and the squirrels have stopped rustling in the brush.

In time, people discover that the animals have died. The trees, too, are becoming gray, and the flowers along the roadside are drooping. All life is dying. People remember the terrible plagues which devastated whole continents in ancient times. In those days, without the aid of science, people were helpless against disease. It seems that such a plague has come now. The people take heart, however, for they have science on their side.

But science has no cure for this plague. In fact, science is the cause of it. The death is caused by a "white granular powder" that has "fallen like snow upon the roofs and the lawns, the fields and the streams."[5] It is a pesticide that people used to fool nature into giving them more crops with less work. The pesticide is called dichloro-diphenyl-trichloro-ethane, or DDT. It has brought the terrible silent spring upon the once-thriving land.

People read the opening fable of *Silent Spring* with horror and fascination. Many took its warning to heart.

They began to consider the possibility of poisoning the environment with chemicals.

Silent Spring was an immediate best-seller. Everyone was talking about it, and everyone had an opinion. A popular TV news show, "CBS Reports," announced that it would devote two programs to "The Silent Spring of Rachel Carson." The show was flooded with mail from interested viewers—even before the programs aired.

Rachel Carson appeared on the show and also found herself spending a great deal of time with reporters from newspapers and other networks. She was pleased that her message was receiving so much publicity, but at the same time she felt annoyed. She was an intensely private woman who shunned the spotlight. Her home on the isolated coast of Maine was no longer a quiet retreat. She had become a public figure.

Rachel Carson dealt with fame as best she could. She received thousands of letters following the publication of *Silent Spring*, and did her best to answer them. Most were from people who thanked her for her carefully researched warning about the direction the industrial world was heading, and who wanted to know what they could do to help.

But not everyone was pleased. Not surprisingly, the pesticide companies didn't much like Rachel Carson. They bitterly protested Carson's assertions that pesticides were harmful to the environment. Many people in government also criticized her. The director of the New Jersey Department of Agriculture called Carson part of a "nature-balancing, organic-gardening, bird-loving, unreasonable citizenry that has not been convinced of the important place of agricultural chemicals in our economy."[6]

Most critics similarly accused Carson of wanting to ban all chemicals. But Rachel Carson did not call for a complete pesticide ban; her point was simply that they should be used with caution. Her book was a detailed examination of the effects of pesticides on the environment. She argued that society should carefully examine each pesticide before allowing it to be sprayed.

Silent Spring stirred much anger, but also a great deal of praise. Nature groups like the Sierra Club gave it their support. Well-known biologists stepped forward to declare that, contrary to the claims of the pesticide companies, Carson's book was scientifically correct.

The *Silent Spring* battle was so furious that it reached the White House even before the book reached the bookstores. At a news conference in August 1962, a few weeks before publication, a reporter asked President John F. Kennedy:

> Mr. President, there appears to be a growing concern among scientists as to the possibility of dangerous long-range side effects from the use of DDT and other pesticides. Have you considered asking the Department of Agriculture or the Public Health Service to take a closer look at this?

To which the President answered:
> Yes, and I know that they already are. I think particularly, of course, since Miss Carson's book, but they are examining the matter.[7]

After that, Washington was abuzz with environmental talk. Many government officials and chemical company experts attacked any suggestions of reducing pesticide use. To them, pesticides were vital to the health of the nation. Trying to stop or reduce the use of pesticides, they claimed, was practically "un-American."

Nevertheless, President Kennedy named a special committee, the President's Science Advisory Committee, to make recommendations about controlling the use of possibly harmful chemicals. Eight months later, the committee issued its report. It recommended that several steps be taken to control the use of pesticides, and it stated quite clearly: "Elimination of the use of persistent toxic pesticides should be the goal."

This was a major step in the fight to avoid a "silent spring" in the United States. The president's committee was quite clear, too, in showing who had led the way. The report said:

"Public literature and the experiences of Panel Members indicate that, until the publication of *Silent Spring* by Rachel Carson, people were generally unaware of the toxicity of pesticides."[8]

The many critics continued to argue, but history had already been changed. The quiet woman with the skillful pen had picked the nation up by its collar and made it see the truth. For the first time, the majority of Americans understood that human beings were changing the planet in harmful ways.

The modern environmental movement had begun.

Maria Carson and her three children:
Marian, Rachel (in her lap), and Robert.

2

The Born Writer

In the nineteenth century, another woman writer had hit a raw nerve in the American psyche and stirred national controversy. In 1852, Harriet Beecher Stowe wrote *Uncle Tom's Cabin*, a novel that exposed the horrors and injustices of slavery. The book divided the nation and contributed to the split that led to the Civil War. President Lincoln admitted as much when, upon meeting Stowe, he said, "So you are the little woman who wrote the book that made this great war."[1] Stowe was a committed abolitionist, a fiery reformer who felt that war was not too high a price to pay to rid the Union of the scourge of slavery.

If President Kennedy had met Rachel Carson, he might have paraphrased Lincoln: "So you are the woman who wrote the book that made this great environmental movement." But Rachel Carson was no fire-breathing reformer. On the contrary, she had worked as a bureaucrat in the government. She had written several best-selling, lyrical books about the sea. And in temperament, she was a private person with just a few very close friends. She was hardly a likely candidate to lead a movement that questioned science, questioned progress, and threatened the profits of industrialists and farmers alike.

And yet . . . from another point of view, everything in Rachel Carson's life pointed like an arrow to *Silent Spring*: her upbringing in a scenic rural community, her education, which developed her natural gifts as a scientist and a poet, and above all, her lifelong, instinctive love of all life around her. Unexpected as it was, *Silent Spring* was also inevitable.

Rachel was born in 1907 in Springdale, Pennsylvania, a quiet little town on a great horseshoe bend of the Allegheny River, about fifteen miles northeast of Pittsburgh. Springdale was an oasis in a grim setting. Pittsburgh at the beginning of this century was already a good example of the environmental devastation that Carson would one day do battle against. It was a sooty, smoke-filled city of steel mills and factories. But its citizens were not alarmed by the gray air and choking fumes. In fact, they were proud of these features, and saw them as symbols of progress and industrialism. They looked at Pittsburgh as an outpost at the forefront of the conquest of nature to satisfy human needs.

Of course, people knew that the city was ugly and smelly, dirty and unpleasant. Pittsburgh was a great place to find work, but no place to live—if you could afford to live elsewhere.

Springdale was elsewhere. It was a pleasant community of about 2,500 people, with rambling Victorian houses and big yards, tree-lined streets, and small farms at the edge of town. The Carson place was one of these: sixty-five acres of wooded hills and pastureland. The "farm" was not actually a farm. The Carsons did not raise any crops or cattle. They had a few farm animals—a cow, a horse, some pigs, and a flock of chickens—and also a garden and an apple orchard.

Rachel's father, Robert, had bought the land as a potential real estate investment. He figured that so much desirable land so close to Pittsburgh would surely one day become a suburban development. When that time came, the family would be rich. But the suburbs didn't expand in the direction of Springdale. Robert Carson's dream never came true.

Though the land never made the Carsons rich, it was the perfect environment for a child who instinctively loved nature. Rachel was the youngest of three children. Her sister Marian was ten and her brother Robert was eight when Rachel was born. Her family was close-knit and somewhat secluded from the community around them. Everyone assumed that the Carsons were very well off—which was not the case at all.

Young Rachel and her dog Candy on the family farm.

Rachel's mother, Maria, was a strong, positive influence on Rachel. In many ways she was more like a partner than a parent. The strong-willed daughter of a Presbyterian minister, Maria McLean had graduated from Washington Female Seminary in 1887. She had studied piano and singing. Perhaps she hoped for a career in music.

But that was not to be. Had Maria lived in a later time, she might have been at the forefront of the women's rights movement. But at the end of the nineteenth century there was little chance for a woman to have a career outside the home. The attitude of society was that a woman's place was in the home, raising children, keeping house, and participating in church and school activities. The very idea of equal rights for women was shocking then. Women would not even be guaranteed the right to vote until the nineteenth amendment to the Constitution took effect in 1920.

One of the few jobs available to women at the time was teaching. Maria chose this as a path to independence, and she was teaching school when she met Robert Carson, who came to town as part of a traveling church quartet. They were married in June 1894, and that was the end of Maria's career. From then on, Maria's duties lay in the home.

Not many people were aware of environmental problems in the early days of the twentieth century. But Maria Carson saw what was happening in nearby Pittsburgh, and she didn't like it. She saw its web of train tracks, its gray factories, and the permanent smog from a thousand smokestacks. She talked to her children about the ugliness and the scarring of the land. She decided that "man was making nature ugly for the best of reasons, and was making his own life ugly."

From the beginning, her youngest child Rachel showed an intellectual curiosity that reflected her mother's concerns. Mother and daughter spent many hours walking together in the fields and orchards of the farm. Young Rachel was delighted by wild bird songs; she wondered at the broad sweep of the sky. She fell in love with the animal stories of Beatrix Potter and the picture books that her mother read to her.

Later, Rachel wrote, "I can remember no times when I wasn't interested in the out-of-doors and the whole world of nature. . . . I was rather a solitary child and spent a great deal of time in the woods and beside streams, learning the birds and the insects and flowers."[2]

Rachel didn't see the ocean until she graduated from college. Years later, people would ask her how, growing up hundreds of miles from the sea, she had decided to become a marine biologist and write books about the ocean. Thinking back, Rachel remembered a conch shell that her mother kept on the table in the Carsons' living room. She recalled holding the shell to her ear and listening to the distant sounds of the ocean, waves breaking and washing onto the sand, the beach wind whispering and echoing. Perhaps the shell and her own vivid imaginings formed her love of the ocean long before she had visited the seashore.

Rachel enjoyed grammar school, especially since she had learned to read early. She began to write short poems, which she made into books that she illustrated and gave to her father. By the time she was ten, she knew that she would be a writer when she grew up. Like many budding writers, she submitted her stories for publication. But unlike most others, she was soon accepted and published.

A children's magazine called *St. Nicholas* encouraged young writers by offering cash prizes for stories. Rachel's first story, "A Battle in the Clouds," won a Silver Badge and a check for $10. She later commented, "I doubt that any royalty check of recent years has given me as great joy as the notice of that award."[3]

Rachel (left) at age 12 with her brother (in his World War I uniform) and sister.

At school, Rachel made a few close friends. In later years some of them said that in order to make friends with Rachel, they first had to be approved by Maria, Rachel's mother. One girl, Charlotte Fisher, was always welcome in the Carson home. Springdale had no library, and Charlotte's family often went to the library in Pittsburgh. Charlotte usually brought back an armload of books for the Carsons.

Nearby lived a family of eight children, the Krumpes. The children's father was Springdale's dentist. Mildred Krumpe became a special friend of Rachel's because they were so much alike. Neither of them was good at sports and games. They would rather read books, write poems, and go for long walks.

Rachel stayed in the same school in Springdale until she was ready for the last two grades of high school. Then she made arrangements to go to Parnassus High School in nearby New Kensington, traveling two miles by streetcar. She was an excellent student there and graduated from Parnassus in 1925 at the head of the class, with a 93.5 average.

Maria was determined that her thoughtful, quiet child would go to college. But how could it be done? The Carsons only seemed to be well-off. In fact, they were "real-estate poor." Robert occasionally sold a lot or two, and the land was always good collateral for loans at the bank. But the family could not afford $1,000 a year for college tuition and expenses. How could Rachel get the higher education she wanted and deserved?

Fortunately, Rachel chose a college that recognized her abilities. She selected Pennsylvania College for Women, in nearby Pittsburgh. It was founded as a Presbyterian liberal arts college for women in 1869. (In 1955 it became coeducational and changed its name to Chatham College.) It had a beautiful campus with long green malls and wooded hills.

Rachel was given a $100 scholarship, which helped. And when the college president, Cora Coolidge, learned about Rachel's circumstances, she arranged an unofficial scholarship of sorts by asking private sources to help pay Rachel's tuition for the first year. It was a gamble based on Rachel's high school performance and the promise that Coolidge saw in her. Perhaps one day the college would boast that Rachel was one of its alumnae. Who could tell? It certainly was worth the few hundreds of dollars it would cost to have her on campus.

When Rachel started college, several facts about her were firmly settled. She loved nature. She loved writing. And she was already the sort of person who could decide for herself what to do and then do it, regardless of what the people around her were doing. Now it was time to enter the wider world.

3

Turning Point

In 1924 President Calvin Coolidge proclaimed, "The chief business of America is business."[1] Americans understood his message and approved. The Roaring Twenties roared forward.

When Rachel started college in 1925, the celebration of American industry had been going on for six years. The country had come out of World War I bitterly opposed to "foreign entanglements." America decided to go its own way. That way was one of production, sales, and consumption. It was the way of big factories, automobiles, radios, steel, and tall buildings. It was the way of progress and prosperity.

This was the era of the flapper (young women who dressed and acted in shockingly "modern" ways), the Charleston (a lively and exuberant new dance), and wild good times. New ways pushed aside stuffy Puritan and Victorian values. People earned good money, spent lavishly, and expected to enjoy themselves.

College was a place to have a good time. Pennsylvania College for Women had an excellent reputation, and many wealthy Pittsburgh families sent their daughters there. Many of the girls had beautiful clothes, partied whenever they wished, and refused to take the academic side of college seriously.

But that was not Rachel Carson's way. She paid no attention whatever to the lifestyles of the day. Her mother

Maria had had a reformer's instincts before the time of reform. Now society was filled with reformers of one kind or another, but Rachel didn't want any part of it. She was at college to study and learn—and that was all. She was there at considerable financial sacrifice to her family. She plunged into the serious side of college life, determined to justify everyone's faith in her abilities.

She made excellent grades from the start, even getting a B-plus in violin, a musical requirement that she had to take but did not really like. (She kept up her lessons, however, and eventually took to playing the violin for relaxation.) Her grades and her reputation as a serious student set her apart. She accepted her superiority with quiet confidence, but never flaunted it. She marched to a different drummer. Later one of her classmates said, "Rachel wasn't antisocial, she just wasn't social." Another said, "She was much more of a scholar than the rest of us. She was well-liked, but never warm . . . not popular, but always respected."[2]

The natural scholar was also a writer. She soon landed a reporter's job on the college paper, *The Arrow*. The paper had a monthly literary supplement called the *Englicode*, which published many of her essays. Two of

Rachel Carson's senior portrait at the Pennsylvania College for Women.

these, "Master of the Ship's Light" and "Cape Arrow-head," show the early yearning of a writer who would become known as "the biographer of the sea." Although she had never seen the ocean the attraction was there.

Once, as she sat in her room at college on a wild and rainy night, a line from the poem "Locksley Hall" by Alfred Lord Tennyson came into her mind:

> *For the night wind arises, roaring seaward,*
>   *and I go.*

Many years later, thinking back on that simple incident, she said, "I can still remember my intense emotional response as that line spoke to something within me, seeming to tell me that my own path led to the sea—which I then had never seen—and that somehow my destiny was linked with the sea."[3]

It seemed unlikely that a writer-to-be, while attending college in land-locked, industrial Pittsburgh, would ever see the ocean. But something happened in her second year at Chatham that changed Rachel's life.

In her sophomore year, Rachel had to meet her science requirement by taking two courses she felt sure she wouldn't enjoy: Biology I and Biology II. She was wrong, however. She liked biology, liked it a lot. It reminded her of her childhood fascination with the bright, changing, cheerful life she had found in the woods and streams near her home.

But biology was a more grown-up version of that fascination, and it answered questions. So *this* is what a flower is made of. So *this* is why trees have leaves. This is how frogs make those funny bass notes. And look at this beautiful, intricate living cell, this paramecium, that isn't visible unless you use a powerful microscope! Biology offered her an endless array of fascinating answers to questions that had long been in the back of her mind. There was no confusion about the answers that biology provided: they were trustworthy facts that people had devoted their lives to exploring.

Rachel had feared that science would be dull and stuffy. But biology was not stuffy at all. Beneath the difficult terminology, Rachel sensed biologists' awe: this is *life*, the biology texts seemed to say, and it is very complex, very beautiful, and it all fits together in wondrous ways.

Rachel had a poet's instincts, but she admired precision, too. Biology clarified, explained, ordered, and made sense out of the life to which she had always reacted with great intensity but without understanding. Despite herself, despite her assumption that she would grow up and become a writer, she was drawn more and more deeply toward the science of life.

Beyond that, her biology teacher, Mary Scott Skinker, was a rare teacher who made her subject beautiful and fascinating. A small, attractive, dynamic woman, she taught with contagious enthusiasm and tapped into Rachel's unacknowledged love of the subject. Rachel's love of biology grew and brought her many hours of agonized self-assessment. She ambled along the neat paths of the college campus, and sat in her room staring out the window, trying to puzzle it out. She had always known that she would be a writer. She was good at writing. She enjoyed writing. But she loved biology. Which path should she choose? How could she be a biologist and a writer too? She had to make a decision.

After many days of pondering, she made up her mind. She would change her major to biology. Her teachers and friends were astounded. Change to biology in her third year? Was she crazy? How would she make up all the required lab work? She would have to spend the rest of her time at college locked up in the laboratory.

Rachel smiled at such concerns. Spending her days in the lab didn't sound so bad to her.

Her decision was particularly disappointing to Professor Grace Croff, her English composition teacher, who looked upon Rachel as her "star." It was probably Mary Scott Skinker's influence that persuaded Rachel to switch. She had become Rachel's mentor, and the two had become close friends. They went on outings together, and spent many hours in the lab. Mary Skinker guided Rachel's exploration of the intricate and fascinating world of biology and helped her see how humans fit into the grand scheme of the earth's ecology.

Rachel was happy. She even began to enjoy other college activities, including athletics. Cool and dependable, she became a goalie on the college's soccer team and made key plays in the 1928 championship game. She was president of Mu Sigma, the college science club, and continued her work on the college newspaper.

In her senior year, Rachel faced the usual problem of money. How would she pay her college tuition? The acreage of her home provided an answer. Her father signed over several lots to Rachel. Rachel in turn used the land as collateral for a loan from the college, to be held until she could repay the debt of $1,600 she owed for her education. The pattern of money problems would continue to haunt Rachel for many years to come. But no one

*Rachel (top, second from right) was a member
of the college field hockey team.*

in her family ever questioned the worth of the education
she had gotten and would continue to get.

During Rachel's senior year, Mary Skinker took a
leave of absence to study for her Ph.D. degree at Johns
Hopkins University. Rachel applied for graduate work at
Johns Hopkins so that they could work together again.

Rachel was awarded her Bachelor of Arts degree in
June 1929, *magna cum laude*— with great honor. It was an
exciting day for Rachel and her parents. But even more
exciting were two other pieces of news: Johns Hopkins
had given her a scholarship to do graduate work there.
And the Pennsylvania College for Women had arranged
a summer study fellowship for Rachel at the Marine
Biological Laboratory at Woods Hole, Massachusetts. At
long last, Rachel was going to see the ocean.

4

I Must Go Down to the Seas

"All aboard!" Rachel Carson stood on the train plat-form, hugged her mother, kissed her father on the cheek, promised to write them, and stepped up onto the train. She found a seat by a window and waved to her parents. Then the whistle sounded, the train lurched, and she was on her way. She was headed to Woods Hole, with a stop to sign up at Johns Hopkins in Maryland and another to visit with Mary Skinker, who had taken ill and was vacationing in Virginia.

The fascination that had come out of nowhere and bound Rachel to biology had taken a turn—toward the sea. She had decided to become a marine biologist be-cause, of all the forms of life she had studied, she found those of the sea the most interesting. As to writing—well, she would have to consider it a hobby rather than a career.

At last the train pulled into Pennsylvania Station in Baltimore, and Rachel made her way to the campus of Johns Hopkins University. She registered for the fall term and met with her adviser, Dr. R. P. Cowles of the zoology department.

The next day she joined Mary Skinker at a Virginia mountain resort. After several days of horseback riding, tennis, and, above all, talk, the two of them traveled to Washington. There Rachel boarded another train, this one to New York City.

She arrived in New York in early morning. She had most of the day to tour the famous island before setting out on the last leg of her journey—by passenger liner along Long Island Sound and up the coast to New Bedford, Massachusetts.

The liner was cheaper than the train. But Rachel chose it because it meant being on the sea. At the start of the journey, a hard July rain was scouring the boat. But Rachel stayed out on deck, entranced by the wonder of Long Island Sound. When the rain stopped she walked around the boat and leaned against the rail, looking and wondering. The liner sailed out into the Atlantic and poked its way, close to shore, up the New England coastline. Looking east, Rachel gazed with awe upon the broad dark ocean, swaying with waves that rolled and broke, farther than the eye could see, for thousands and thousands of miles. She remembered the words of John Masefield's poem "Sea-Fever":

> *I must go down to the seas again,*
> *to the lonely sea and the sky,*
> *And all I ask is a tall ship*
> *and a star to steer her by,*
> *And the wheel's kick and the wind's song*
> *and the white sails shaking,*
> *And a grey mist on the sea's face*
> *and a grey dawn breaking.*[1]

At New Bedford, Rachel transferred to another boat that took her to Woods Hole. The Marine Biological Laboratory at Woods Hole—referred to as the MBL—was a branch of the U.S. Bureau of Fisheries, which offered summer courses in marine biology. (Woods Hole was also soon to be the home of the Oceanographic Institution, which was endowed by the Rockefeller Institution in 1930. Together they would form one of the largest and most prestigious marine research centers in the world.)

And so began six weeks which Rachel later described as "the happiest days of my life." Her main task was to work on a paper that her Hopkins advisor Dr. Cowles had recommended about the cranial nerves of the turtle and the terminal nerves in lizards, snakes, and "maybe crocodiles." The MBL was a paradise for a young scholar. Its library seemed to have everything ever written about the ocean. The laboratories had all the latest and best equipment, and there were seawater tanks and chemically preserved specimens showing thousands of forms of sea life. Scientists who were authorities on oceanographic science were all around her, always willing to talk to a promising young graduate student. And, of course, right outside the door was the Great Laboratory, the Atlantic Ocean.

Rachel did a lot of field work, combing the beaches, exploring salt marshes and tide pools, wading in the ocean, searching caves, and collecting specimens. There was also time for picnics and shopping in town with Mary Frye, a friend from college with whom she shared a room at a boarding house. Rachel spent her spare time studying German, a language requirement of Johns Hopkins University.

When summer was over, a suntanned, freckled, happy young woman said reluctant good-byes to the people she had met and worked with. The stay at Woods Hole had erased the last doubts Rachel felt about becoming a marine biologist. She had gone to the ocean, and it had welcomed her.

When fall came and Rachel started graduate school, the Carson family had to make some changes. The stock market crash of 1929 was followed by the Great Depression, and the American economy went into a tailspin. Rachel's father's dream of making his fortune in real estate was now clearly hopeless. Rachel found a house in Stammer's Run, Maryland, and persuaded the family to move into quarters better suited to the economic hard times they faced.

Everybody had jobs to do. Her father found work in Baltimore. Her mother did the cooking and housekeeping, and Rachel found a job as a lab assistant at Johns Hopkins in addition to a part-time teaching position in the biology department at the University of Maryland. Her brother Robert rejoined the family when his business in Pittsburgh failed, and he also found work in Baltimore.

One day, Robert took a cat named Mitzi in partial payment for some radio repair work he had done. Mitzi was the first of a long dynasty of cats that remained in the Carson household for years to come and became Rachel's writing companions. Rachel was to develop the habit of doing her writing late at night. There was always a cat in the room to keep her company, messing up the neatly stacked typescripts or batting at the typewriter keys with its paws.

In June 1932, Rachel Carson received her Master's Degree from Johns Hopkins. Now it was time to find full-time work. She decided to visit Elmer Higgins, a member of the Bureau of Fisheries, with whom she had had an interview once before. Although Higgins had not been very helpful and had suggested that there were few jobs for woman scientists at the Bureau, he had been friendly and direct.

Her second interview went better. Higgins had been given an assignment to write fifty-two scripts for a series of radio broadcasts about the work of the Bureau. He was an eminent biologist, but no writer. On the other hand, few good writers knew much about marine biology. And no one seemed to be able to make the Bureau's work sound exciting—or even very interesting.

After chatting with Carson for a while, Higgins asked, "Oh, by the way, can you write?" He explained the project, and said that the Bureau needed someone who knew the field and could also write. Carson said she was willing to try.

The radio programs were called "Romance Under the Waters," although the Bureau had nicknamed them "Seven-Minute Fish Tales." They glamorized the many inhabitants of the ocean and the Bureau's work in regulating fish harvests and conserving ocean resources. Rachel Carson plunged into writing scripts, and Higgins was very pleased with them. His gamble on hiring a woman scientist had worked out perfectly. Carson's scripts were so good that he decided to rework them a little and publish them as a government booklet. He asked her to write an introduction for it, but when she turned it in, Higgins did not think it would do. Carson was upset and asked what was wrong with it.

Nothing was wrong with it, Higgins told her. The problem was that the work was simply too good. He encouraged Carson to submit it to the *Atlantic Monthly* magazine.

Carson mumbled her thanks for the compliment. She could not imagine that the *Atlantic Monthly*, which had published the work of literary giants like Thoreau and Emerson, would be interested in her writing. She took the manuscript home, and dropped it into a desk drawer.

Carson loved her work at the Bureau, but it was part-time and paid only $19.25 a week. Even combined with her teaching assistant salary, it did not provide enough money. Then death struck the family—twice. In July 1935, her father, Robert, died. The following year her older sister Marian died. Marian had been ill for several years, and upon her death her two little girls, Marian and Marjorie, were left in the Carsons' care. It was a time of grief and mourning. Financial troubles were also piling up. Rachel Carson needed a full-time job, and she very much hoped to get one in the Bureau of Fisheries.

In 1936 a position as junior aquatic biologist opened up in the Bureau. Carson took the department's examination and achieved the highest score. Elmer Higgins happily offered her the job. Technically, she had the rank of biologist, but Higgins was well aware of her writing ability. She was hired at a salary of $2,000 a year and assigned as assistant editor in the Information Division.

Carson now began to do freelance writing to supplement her income. The Sunday editor of the *Baltimore Sun* had read the pamphlet based on her radio scripts and asked her to write something for the paper. Rachel wrote an article about commercial shad fishing in the Chesapeake Bay, where dumping of industrial and municipal wastes and destructive fishing practices threatened to kill off all the shad. The editor liked her work, and Rachel became an occasional contributor to the *Sun*.

Carson felt encouraged about her writing. One day, while rummaging through her desk, she came across the introduction she had written for Elmer Higgins. She re-read it. Why not send it to the *Atlantic Monthly*, as Higgins had suggested? At worst she would have another rejection slip to add to the pile she had accumulated. She reworked the copy a little, titled it "Undersea," slipped it into an envelope, and dropped it in the mail.

One evening a few weeks later she arrived home. Her mother was holding an envelope. It was from the *Atlantic Monthly*. Rachel tore it open. Inside was a letter and a check for $75.00! Rachel was thrilled.

"Undersea" came out in September 1937. It was the first time that a large audience of literate but nonscientific readers had encountered Rachel Carson's wonderful blend of lyrical writing and hard facts.

Carson commented later that from her article in the *Atlantic*, "everything else followed." Not long after its publication, she got a letter from Quincy Howe, the editor-in-chief of Simon and Schuster, asking if she would like to write a book for his company. This was followed by a letter from the famous historian and writer Hendrik Willem van Loon. He praised her *Atlantic* essay and said that he had pointed it out to Quincy Howe. Indeed, Van Loon and Howe had exchanged letters about the piece, and both knew that they had found a talented naturalist-writer. Later the two men had a good-humored, ongoing argument about which one had dis-covered Rachel Carson.

They urged Carson to write a book about the sea. Perhaps unconsciously she had been dreaming all along about such a book, because she immediately knew what she would write. She would tell about each part of the sea, about its beauty and mystery and terror, and she would do it through the eyes of its inhabitants: the black skimmer, the mackerel, and others. She would tread a delicate line, making the creatures neither too human nor too abstract. People would understand the creatures and the sea by experiencing the creatures' lives.

The more she thought about it, the more excited she became. One day in January 1938 she traveled to Van Loon's house in Old Greenwich, Connecticut, to discuss her ideas for the book with the two men. Both were enthusiastic, and encouraged her to start at once.

Carson still put in at least eight hours a day at the office. But at night she wrote the first chapter and an outline of the rest of the book and sent it to Howe at Simon and Schuster. After what seemed quite a long time, a letter came back with an advance check for $250 and a note from Howe encouraging her to get on with the writing as quickly as possible.

In the meantime, Carson had written articles for the *Baltimore Sun*. She reread them and found that much of her work could be used in the new book if it were rewritten and worked into the new format. She set to work.

She discovered a lot about writing. She found she was not a fast writer. The right words did not come easily to her. When the house was quiet and everybody was asleep, she sat down at her desk and stroked the cat. "It's just you and me, Mitzi," she would say. She once said, "Writing is a lonely occupation at best . . . during the actual work of creation, the writer cuts himself off from all others and confronts his subject alone"[2]—except for a friendly cat.

The book, which she titled *Under the Sea Wind*, was illustrated by Howard French, a staff artist of the *Baltimore Sun*. It was published in November 1941 and dedicated to Rachel's mother, Maria, who had encouraged her so strongly and who typed the final manuscript.

Some critics consider *Under the Sea Wind* Carson's finest book. It certainly showed her talent at presenting scientific facts with grace and conviction and building vivid pictures through the accumulation of sharp details. Moreover, it could transport readers not only to strange places but right into the lives of creatures they had never thought about before. In the following excerpt, Carson describes an encounter between a mackerel she calls Scomber and a two-hundred-pound rock cod.

Moving along above the ledge, Scomber suddenly came upon a six-foot rock cod, a two-hundred-pound monster of his kind, who lived on the ledge among the rockweeds. The cod had grown old and very large because of his cunning. He had found the rock ledge above the deep pit of the sea years before and, knowing it instinctively for a good hunting place, he had adopted the ledge for his own, fiercely driving away the other cod. He spent much of his time lying on the ledge, which was in deep purple shadow after the sun had passed the zenith. From this lair he could move out suddenly to seize fishes as they roved along the rock wall. Many fishes met their death in his jaws, among them cunners and hook-eared sculpins, sea ravens with ragged fins, flounder and sea robins, blennies and skates.

Sight of the young mackerel roused the cod from the semitorpor in which he had lain since the last feeding time and kindled his hunger. He swung his heavy body out from the ledge and climbed steeply to the shoal. Scomber fled before him.[3]

There is a story, other than the one between its covers, about *Under the Sea Wind*. It was published in November 1941 and was well-received by the critics and the scientific community. It became a selection of the Scientific Book Club, and had strong sales—for the first two weeks.

Then on December 7, 1941, the Japanese attacked Pearl Harbor, and the United States was plunged into World War II. The shocked nation had no time for a poetically realistic book about the sea. Sales of all books plummeted. *Under the Sea Wind* sold about 1,600 copies in its short life and was then all but forgotten. The press run was sold off and the publisher lost interest. Today a copy of the 1941 edition of *Under the Sea Wind* sells for $150, but in 1941 no one was interested.

5

Triumph

"I am convinced that writing a book is a very poor gamble financially," Rachel Carson wrote in 1942. "This is based not only on my own experience (which, heaven knows, confirms it fully) but on what friends in the publishing business tell me. The average book will earn its author very little more than one magazine article placed with the 'right' magazine."[1]

Carson was, to say the least, disillusioned with the rewards of writing books, no matter how satisfying the writing had been. The three years of working at night and on weekends on *Under the Sea Wind* had made her less than $1,000.

Very well. Life went on. The family needed to be supported. And the Bureau, now called the Fish and Wildlife Service, had to do its part in the war effort.

Carson's part was to help persuade Americans that fish were a suitable and healthy substitute for the red meat that had to be sent to the theaters of war. She wrote a long series of pamphlets on the preparation of seafoods. These were very popular, and the Bureau sent thousands of the brochures through the mails in answer to requests. The idea of Carson's writing seafood recipes was very amusing to her co-workers, who knew that she loathed cooking and doing housework. Her mother Maria did the cooking and housework in the Carson household.

Soon, however, she got a chance to do some writing

of a more significant nature. The Fish and Wildlife Service was to produce a series of booklets called *Conservation in Action*, and Rachel Carson was chosen to write and edit several of them. The title of the series suggests that in the 1940s there was already some concern about preserving the natural world. While most people were ignorant of the ways humans were changing their environment, there was a long tradition of writers and naturalists who warned of coming dangers. In the nineteenth century, the American writers Ralph Waldo Emerson and Henry David Thoreau had argued that the United States must not try to abandon the natural world in its quest for industrial development.

Then, in the latter part of the nineteenth century, John Muir hiked from the Midwest to the Gulf of Mexico, and fell in love with the American landscape. He became a passionate defender of the natural world, and he argued in favor of establishing a forest conservation policy. In 1903, he got his wish. President Theodore Roosevelt signed a law that established the National Park Service. It was the first solid sign of government involvement in conservation.

In the 1930s, another step was taken with Aldo Leopold's work on wildlife management. Leopold argued that the nation's populations of game animals— such as deer, bear, birds, and fish—had to be managed or those species would eventually become extinct. Leopold's work helped guide state governments to manage their animal populations. One result of this work was the passage of the Migratory Bird Conservation Act. After the act was passed, hundreds of wildlife refuges were set up. Rachel Carson's *Conservation in Action* booklets described how these refuges helped to preserve wildlife.

Carson wrote about half of the dozen booklets produced. She introduced the series with a paragraph that was adopted as a creed by the U.S. Fish and Wildlife Service and was printed in many of its publications about its sanctuary programs:

> Wild creatures, like men, must have a place to live. As civilization creates cities, builds highways, and drains marshes, it takes away, little by little, the land that is suitable for wildlife. As their spaces for living dwindle, the wildlife populations themselves decline.[2]

Carson on Hawk Mountain in Pennsylvania.

Research for *Conservation in Action* called for work in the field. In the late 1940s, Carson finally had the chance to get out of the office. She and a new friend, Shirley Briggs, traveled to the Chincoteague Refuge on an island off the Virginia coast to gather material for her first booklet. She spent ten days on the *Albatross III*, a fishing trawler converted to a research ship, helping to do a census of the fish off Georges Bank, south of Nova Scotia. She also traveled to Plum Island, off the coast of Massachusetts, and to the Mattamuskeet Refuge near North Carolina, where she observed the wintering whistling swans.

She returned to Woods Hole, too, where she combed the beach along the Atlantic coast and waded in the tidal pools—experiences she would communicate vividly in later books. And she even learned deep-sea diving around the Florida Keys, which was a real accomplishment in those days, when diving called for huge helmets, bulky rubber suits, and lead weights.

Promotions came rapidly, and by 1947 she was editor-in-chief of the Service's Information Division. As editor she was fair, but also very demanding. She expected the same carefully crafted and accurate work from others that she did herself. Bob Hines, a department staff artist who later illustrated *The Edge of the Sea*, remembered her as a "very able executive. . . . She knew how to get things done the quickest, simplest, most direct way. . . . She was just so doggone good she couldn't see why other people couldn't try to be the same. She had *standards*, high ones."[3]

In spite of the meager financial rewards of her first book, the desire to write stayed with her. She had become a successful part-time freelance writer, published in magazines such as *Collier's, Coronet,* and *Nature.* But she felt caught in a web of responsibilities and small successes. At one point, she wrote to a friend:

> No, my life isn't at all well ordered and I don't know where I am going! I know that if I could choose what seems to me the ideal existence, it would be just to live by writing. And all the while my job with the Service grows and demands more and more of me, leaving less time that I could put on my own writing. And as my salary increases little by little, it becomes even more impossible to give up! That is my problem right now, and not knowing what to do about it, I do nothing.[4]

The urge to write another book about the sea had been with her for some time and was growing stronger. She knew what she wanted to write: a book that "I myself searched for on library shelves but never found." It would be a book that explored every age of the ocean, from its surface to the very depths and mysteries of its floor. It would be a biography of the ocean.

A biography of the ocean? Yes, it was logical. Suppose you wanted to learn about an important person. How would you do it? You would go to the biography section of the library and take out a book that tells you the person's life story. Well, nothing on earth was more interesting to Rachel Carson than the ocean. But she had never found a book that told its story. So she would write it: the ocean's birth, its early years, its growth and

The biologist at work.

changes, what the ocean is today and how it came to be that way.

She felt the need for this book so strongly that, despite her skepticism about books as a source of income, she began the monumental task of researching a book she intended to call *Return to the Sea*. In the next three years, the title would be changed many times: *Mother Sea, Biography of the Sea, The Story of the Sea, The Empire of the Sea,* and *Sea Without End* were all considered. Commenting wryly on the search, she wrote, "The perfect book title seems to be still evading us, and I have an unhappy feeling that we will think of it about publication day. Current suggestions from irreverent friends and relatives include 'Out of My Depth' and 'Carson at Sea.' "[5]

She knew that some writers work best when they have a literary agent, a person hired to approach publishers with a manuscript and help negotiate a contract. The right agent is like a friend and a lawyer, an ally who is objective, on your side, and looking out for your best interests. After interviewing several people, she selected Marie Rodell as her agent. Rodell had experience both as a writer and a publishing executive, and recognized Carson's exceptional ability. When Carson had finished about a third of the manuscript and had a firm outline for the rest, Rodell negotiated a contract with Oxford University Press, where Philip Vaudrin became Carson's editor. Then, at last, a title was chosen: *The Sea Around Us.*

The last half of 1948 and all of 1949 became a time of agonizing, pressured writing. Carson returned to her old routine of long ago, commuting to her job during the day and settling down at night, in the company of her new cat, Muffin, to work on the book. She faced the blank page alone, and waited, and wrote, and listened with her acute writer's ear . . . and rewrote again until it was right.

There were no models for this book—no writer had ever attempted to do what she was doing. Her subject matter was nothing less than the ocean itself, in all its ancient grandeur. But the particular facts were buried in obscure texts and scientific papers and in the correspondence she was carrying on with marine biologists and oceanographers all over the world. She had to translate the dry facts into prose that glowed, was alive, and sang. It was slow going.

Carson had bought a new home in Silver Spring, Maryland, so the family had to move, and her responsibilities at work were growing. And there was the Oxford deadline—May 1950—to meet. Fortunately her financial problems were lightened when she received a fellowship from the Eugene F. Saxton Memorial, which was established to give financial help to worthy writers. Night by night, the manuscript grew. She made her due date.

It was obvious to Marie Rodell and to Philip Vaudrin at Oxford that chapters from the book would make excellent articles for a magazine. There would be benefits to everyone if it could be arranged: money for the author, publicity for the book, and larger book sales. One chapter, "Birth of an Island," was published in the *Yale Review* in December. It was later awarded a $1,000 prize as the best science writing of 1950. Then Rodell ran out of luck. Other chapters were turned down by *Harper's, Saturday Evening Post, National Geographic,* and a dozen other magazines.

At last Edith Oliver, a *New Yorker* editor, read several chapters and showed them enthusiastically to William Shawn, the editor-in-chief of the magazine. He loved

Carson taking notes by the shore.

them. In the spring of 1951,*The New Yorker* published about half of the book in a series of three articles called "Profiles of the Sea."

The *New Yorker* profiles had an enormous effect on Rachel Carson's career. *The New Yorker* was a very prestigious magazine. When *The Sea Around Us* was published, on July 2, 1951, an eager audience was waiting to find out what happened in the other half of the book.

Oxford University Press had been too conservative in its estimate of the number of books to print, and it was caught short immediately. Booksellers found it difficult to keep the book in stock. The publisher happily went back to press and printed more copies. The book entered the best-seller list in July, topped it in September, and remained on it for eighty-three weeks.

The Sea Around Us had universal appeal. It was not a book for specialists. It had all the validity and care of a scientific text, but it also had simplicity and poetry. The *New York Times* summarized the impact appeal of the book: "Great poets from Homer down to Masefield have tried to evoke the deep mystery and endless fascination of the ocean, but the . . . gentle Miss Carson seems to have the best of it. Once or twice in a generation does the world get a physical scientist with literary genius. Miss Carson has written a classic in *The Sea Around Us*."[6]

The following passage shows why. In her first book, *Under the Sea Wind*, Carson had created a magical world through the accumulation of carefully formed images. In her second book, she taught scientific concepts with lucidity and grace. Many readers remarked that once they began the book, they could not put it down until they had read every word. They were drawn into the story by the charm and force of her words, images, and thoughts. In one passage, she explained that the sea once occupied places far, far away from today's ocean.

You do not have to travel to find the sea, for the traces of its ancient stands are everywhere about. Though you may be a thousand miles inland, you can easily find remainders that will reconstruct for the eye and ear of the mind the processions of its ghostly waves and the roar of its surf, far back in time. So, on a mountaintop in Pennsylvania, I have sat on rocks of whitened limestone, fashioned of the shells of billions upon billions of minute sea creatures. Once they had lived and died in an arm of the ocean that overlay this place, and their limy remains had settled to the bottom. There, after eons of time, they had become compacted into rock and the sea had receded; after yet more eons the rock had been uplifted by bucklings of the earth's crust and now it formed the backbone of a long mountain range.[7]

Before that book fell away from the best-seller list, Rachel Carson had the intense satisfaction of seeing its earlier sibling, *Under the Sea Wind*, join it there. In April of 1952, Oxford reissued her first book, and the people who had read *The Sea Around Us* discovered its twin, alike in its skilled lyricism, different in its content and the worlds it created. The two books established Rachel Carson as America's leading nature writer, a woman whose compelling words would always find an audience.

6

The Writer's Life

Fame and fortune are words that most people think of as being positive. Fortune was, of course, welcome to Carson. But since she was an intensely private person, fame had its downside. She wrote about experiences she had while promoting her best-seller:

> . . . [I]t had never occurred to me . . . that people would go to great lengths just to have a look at someone whose book was a best seller. A few months after *The Sea* was published, I was on a long southern field trip for my new book. In a strange town, I went into a beauty shop, and while I was sitting under the drier—which until then I had considered an inviolate sanctuary— the proprietor came over, turned off the drier, and said: "I hope you don't mind, but there is someone who wants to meet you." I admit I felt hardly at my best, with a towel around my neck and my hair in pin curls. At another place during the same trip, a knock came at the door of our motor court early one morning. When my mother opened the door, a determined woman pushed past her and presented two books for autographing to an author who was still abed and, if the truth must be told, very much annoyed.[1]

By September, *The Sea Around Us* was at the top of the best-seller list. It remained on the list for a year and a half. In November, Carson signed the one-hundred-thousandth copy sold at a department store in Cleveland. By March of the following year, sales passed two hundred thousand copies. The book was translated into more than thirty languages, so that it became an international best-seller as well. Carson received several honorary degrees, including one from her alma mater, the Pennsylvania College for Women, as a Doctor of Literature. And the book won the National Book Award for the best nonfiction book of 1951.

Rachel Carson, government employee, serious scientist, and something of a loner, was suddenly a celebrity.

Carson in her office at her home in Maine.

She was in constant demand for speaking engagements, in-store book autographing parties, award ceremonies, honorary degree receptions. For a while, she cooperated. But eventually she rebelled, writing to Marie Rodell, "In Cleveland and Pittsburgh, I was left at the mercy of a bunch of eager beavers who thought of how many minutes the day contained and how many events they could cram into it, and as a result I came home in a state of exhaustion. I will not submit to anything like that again."[2] And at the award ceremony at the Pennsylvania College for Women, she confided to a friend that she felt much more comfortable in sneakers at the shore than in high heels at a reception.

Fortunately, there was more work to be done of the kind that Carson enjoyed. Houghton Mifflin Company, which produced a highly respected series of nature guides, had contacted her while she was still working on *The Sea Around Us* and asked if she would do a guide to life on the seashore. She had agreed.

Most nature guides list, describe, and show pictures of life forms of an area. People use them to help identify the life they see there. Carson wanted to do more than that. She thought of the book as series of brief biological sketches that would put each living creature into its biological context, showing "why it lives where it does, how it has adapted its structures and habitat to its environment, how it gets food, its life cycle, its enemies, competitors, associates."[3]

Now Carson was ready to try out her dream of actually making a living from her writing. She had requested a year's leave of absence from the U.S. Fish and Wildlife Service, to begin in June 1951. She plunged into the mountain of research that would need to be done before actually writing the book. Soon she was completely immersed in the new book, so that when the choruses of praise came upon publication of *The Sea Around Us*, she felt curiously detached from it all. That book was like a child whom she had raised and sent into the world. It was thriving and she was proud of it, and she would do what she could to make certain it did well. But meanwhile, back at home, another book needed careful nurturing and bringing up. That was where her heart lay now.

Her year's leave of absence was spent in expeditions to beaches from Maine to the Florida Keys. As it came to an end, she realized that she could not go back to her old routine of working all day at the office and writing at night and on weekends. Besides, she did not have to. *The Sea Around Us* had made enough money so that at long last her dream of being an independent writer could be realized. In June 1952, she resigned her position at the U.S. Fish and Wildlife Service and took up writing fulltime.

Carson toiled away at the guide to shore life, but nothing quite seemed to work. Slowly it dawned on her how the book must be written. Almost two years after she had signed the contract, she wrote to her editor that "the attempt to write a structureless chapter that was just one little thumbnail biography after another was driving me mad."[4] She suggested a completely different plan for this book. She would write about how all of the life forms in one place interrelated to form something called an "ecosystem." She would write the first popular book on ecology.

Today "ecology" is almost as familiar as the word "environment." But in the early 1950s it was an obscure scientific term describing the study of the relationships of all organisms to each other and to their physical surroundings. The concept was very abstract.

Carson thought that the seashore would be the ideal place to introduce such concepts, for here, especially at the tidal zone, life had to adapt to the characteristics of both the land and the sea. How does life adjust to two severely different environments: the sand, sun, and air of low tide, and the inrushing seawaters of high tide? What communities are formed? How do they survive in a world that goes topsy-turvy twice a day, as the tides roll in and out?

Carson described three different ecosystems on the eastern coast of the United States: the rocky shore from Maine to Cape Cod, the sandy beaches from there to South Carolina, and the coral and mangrove shores from Georgia to the Florida Keys.

Chapter by chapter the book was written. As with *The Sea Around Us*, chapters were excerpted and published in *The New Yorker*. And as with that book, *The Edge of the Sea* received splendid reviews. It became a best-seller in 1955. Carson's natural lyricism and her scientific accuracy once again blended together perfectly to enchant the general reader and the scientist alike. In the following passage, she describes a creature that lives in the Florida Keys, on the wreck of coral rock that lies on the shore.

These deeply eroded rocks are the home of the chitons, whose primitive form harks back to some ancient group of mollusks of which they are the only living representatives. Their oval bodies, covered with a jointed shell of eight trans-verse plates, fit into depressions in the rocks when the tide is out. They grip the rocks so strongly that even heavy waves can get no hold on their sloping contours. When the high tide covers them, they begin to creep about, resuming their rasping of vegetation from the rocks, their bodies swaying to and fro in time to the scraping motions of the radula or file-like tongue. Month in and month out, a chiton moves only a few feet in any direction; because of this sedentary habit, the spores of algae and the larvae of barnacles and tube-building worms settle upon its shell and develop there. Sometimes, in dark wet caves, the chitons pile up, one on top of another, and each scrapes algae off the back of the one beneath it. In a small way these primitive mollusks may be an agent of geologic change as they feed on the rocks, each removing, along with the algae, minute scrapings of rock particles and so, over the centuries and the millennia in which this ancient race of beings has lived its simple life, contributing to the processes of erosion by which earth surfaces are worn away.[5]

Carson was now 48 years old and seemed to have arrived at a secure and serene stage of life. She was internationally known and honored for her authoritative and beautifully written books. She had always loved the wild land at the edge of the ocean in Maine, and in 1953 she bought an acre and a half of land overlooking the wild seashore in West Southport, near Sheepscot Bay. She built a summer cottage there. The ocean was literally at her front door, and a forest of pine and hemlock was her backyard. For the rest of her life, this was her real home, even though it was only a summer cabin. The Maine coast was her laboratory and sanctuary, her source of information and inspiration. She was living in Maine, next to her beloved sea. She could look forward to many years of relaxed and prosperous work as a writer. She felt that she had written herself out about the ocean, but there were still the continents to consider.

A New York publisher asked if Carson might be interested in doing a book about evolution. She considered it, and then decided against taking the project.

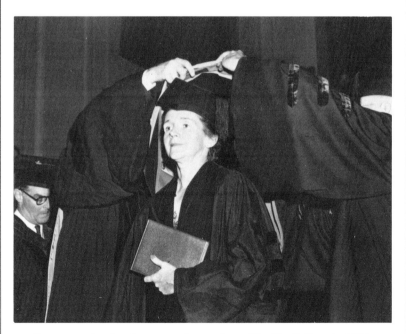

Carson received an honorary degree from Oberlin College in 1951.

She wrote a script for a TV program called "Something About the Sky." She briefly considered making a large anthology of sea-related pieces. She indulged a new-found hobby: taking photographs through a microscope. She deepened her friendships with people in Maine and corresponded with leading naturalists throughout the world. She answered the hundreds of letters people wrote after reading her books.

It truly seemed that her life had found its pattern and had settled into a peaceful groove. But that was not so. In fact, all her work, success, fame, and talents—all the poetry she had written and all the research she had done until now—had only been training and preparation.

In January 1958, a woman named Olga Huckins sent her a copy of a letter. Huckins had originally sent it to a newspaper, the *Boston Herald*, which had published it. Now she wanted Rachel Carson to see it.

That letter would change Carson's life. In time, it would come to change America's attitudes about the environment.

7

Hidden Catastrophes

Olga Huckins and her husband were friends of Carson's who had property just north of Cape Cod in Massachusetts, which they had made into a bird sanctuary. In the summer of 1957, the area had been heavily sprayed with DDT to control mosquitoes. Huckins described what happened in her letter to the *Boston Herald*:

To the Editor of the *Herald*:

Mr. R. C. Codman, who wrote that he "is actively associated" with the Commonwealth of Mass. aerial spraying programs for alleged mosquito control, also says that state tests have proved that the mixture used—fuel oil with DDT—last summer over Plymouth and Barnstable Counties was entirely harmless.

These testers must have used black glasses, and the trout that did not feel the poison were super-fish. . . .

The mosquito control plane flew over our small town last summer. Since we live close to the marshes, we were treated to several lethal doses as the pilot crisscrossed our place. And we consider the spraying of active poison over private land to be a serious aerial intrusion.

The "harmless" shower bath killed seven of our lovely songbirds outright. We picked up three dead bodies the next morning right by the door. They were birds that had lived close to us, trusted us, and built their nests in our trees year after year. The next day, three were scattered around the bird bath. (I had emptied it and scrubbed it after the spraying but YOU CAN NEVER KILL DDT.) On the following day one robin dropped suddenly from a branch in our woods. We were too heartsick to hunt for other corpses. All of these birds died horribly, and in the same way. Their bills were gaping open, and their splayed claws were drawn up to their breasts in agony.

Mr. Codman also says that between DDT and mosquitoes, he prefers DDT. We had no choice, we have had both. All summer long, every time we went into the garden, we were attacked by the most voracious mosquitoes that had ever appeared there. But the grasshoppers, visiting bees, and other harmless insects, were all gone.

The remedy of this situation is not to double the strength of the spray and come again. It is to STOP THE SPRAYING OF POISONS FROM THE AIR everywhere until all the evidence, biological and scientific, immediate and long run, of the effects upon wild life and human beings are known.

Air spraying where it is not needed or wanted is inhuman, undemocratic, and probably unconstitutional. For those of us who stand helplessly on the tortured earth, it is intolerable.

Olga Owens Huckins, Duxbury[1]

In fact, more sprayings were planned. Huckins enclosed a note with the copy of the letter asking Carson for names of people in Washington to contact. Carson was as appalled as her friend at the wanton poisoning. She decided to look into the spraying programs. For several weeks she telephoned and wrote letters, trying to find out about the pesticide policies of the government. The more she learned, the more horrified and angry she became.

The government officials did not have the slightest intention of stopping the spraying programs. If anything, they had ambitious plans to increase them. They said that they were certain the insecticides were harmless and had no bad side effects. They said that the chemicals did their jobs and then simply disappeared. They dismissed people like Huckins as hysterical nature mystics who preferred birds over people. They had no plans to do research to find out what the further effects of massive sprayings might be.

But they did have plans. The government was preparing to buy and use even more powerful "-cides" to deal with insects that refused to die and came back stronger than ever after being sprayed. The officials said that the success and prosperity of American farming depended on the use of insecticides and herbicides. And they implied that anyone who questioned them was against progress, against people being fed, and against "the American way."

Rachel Carson was a naturalist who had spent her whole career teaching that life is a complicated, interrelated web. She knew that you could not change one part without affecting all the rest. Did these officials really believe that they could indiscriminately soak the land with a billion gallons of DDT, and even more powerful pesticides, and not poison the land and the life on it and around it?

Carson recognized that "everything that meant most to me as a naturalist was being threatened."[2] She wrote a description of an article on the dangers of overuse of DDT and asked Marie Rodell to find out if any of the

DDT being sprayed over a forest of fir trees in Idaho.

national magazines would be interested in it. None were. *Good Housekeeping*, for instance, said: "It is our feeling that the article proposed by Miss Rodell is something which we should under no circumstances consider. We doubt whether many of the things outlined in this letter could be substantiated."[3]

In May 1957, the U.S. Department of Agriculture and the New York Department of Agriculture and Markets announced plans for massive DDT spraying of parts of Long Island to eradicate gypsy moths. Carson was outraged. She knew that the gypsy moth lived in forests, not in the meadows and gardens of Long Island. A group of citizens went to court to try to stop the spraying. Their petition was denied, and the spraying took place as scheduled.

Then the citizens went back to court seeking a permanent injunction, a court order that would forbid further spraying. Carson wrote to the renowned writer E. B. White, who worked for *The New Yorker*, suggesting that he report on the trial for the magazine. He wrote back that she herself ought to do it; she was as qualified as he was to write on the environment.

Perhaps she would. Perhaps she could rouse the public's awareness with a magazine article in *The New Yorker* and a short book for Houghton Mifflin. The article would be about the Long Island trial, which ultimately went against the citizens. The book would be a collection of essays. *The New Yorker* agreed to publish an article of twenty thousand to thirty thousand words, and her publisher agreed to the short book. In May 1958, she signed a contract for the book, to be completed in July and published in January 1959.

Carson soon understood that in order to succeed the book would involve an enormous amount of research, and it would have to be superbly written. Some had written moving books that protested the indiscriminate use of pesticides, but they had not done careful research and the books were dismissed as "unscientific." Some had written carefully researched indictments that were earnest, but they were dull and therefore went unread. It was Elmer Higgins's old problem with the "fish-story" radio scripts: the job needed someone who knew the field and could write. Carson knew that she was that person.

She set out to learn more about the field. She began to accumulate materials in a wide number of sciences: medicine, land use, organic chemistry, agronomy, and many other areas. Each piece of knowledge seemed to lead in other directions; each fact suggested other areas of research.

She loved to do research—in fact, she preferred it to the actual writing, which was always agony for her. She wrote letters to authorities on pesticides, and was answered with a deluge of mail. She enlisted the help of friends she had made at the Long Island trial, and they flooded her with sources and papers. She went to the library to study journals and papers, even staying away from her beloved house in Maine until late summer. She contacted friends in Washington, who put her in touch with others, who knew yet others.

July 1—Carson's deadline—came and went, and her editor, Paul Brooks, saw that once again, just as with *The Edge of the Sea*, this was a book that would take time, would evolve, and would quite possibly be another masterpiece. He gave her the extra time.

In the midst of the painstaking research, her mother Maria died in December 1958, at the age of 89. Maria had always been at her daughter's side, keeping house, cooking, typing manuscripts, packing for trips. Through all the crises, fatigue, and tragic deaths, Maria had always been there, supportive and proud. Now she was gone. Carson mourned deeply, but by February she was back into the research for the book that was becoming more and more important for her.

The research turned up one horror story after another. Typical was the U.S. Department of Agriculture's 1957 program to eradicate the fire ant. Fire ants had entered the southeastern United States some forty years before from South America. They did not destroy crops, but they had a nasty, though relatively harmless, sting. In fact, the insect was not even mentioned in a 1957 Department bulletin on agricultural pests. Nonetheless, the USDA decided to eradicate this "despoiler of southern agriculture and killer of birds and livestock and man."[4]

In 1958, the USDA sprayed one million acres across the South with dieldrin and heptachlor, both many times more powerful than DDT. The heartbreaking devastation of wildlife and birds was so obvious that many citizens protested the spraying. They might have saved their breath. The USDA knew best. The program went forward, the devastation continued. The ants hesitated momentarily, adapted to the poison, and continued their northward progress. By 1961, the program had slowly died out.

Carson wrote, "Never has any pesticide program been so thoroughly and deservedly damned by practically everyone except the beneficiaries of this 'sales bonanza' (the pesticide companies). It is an outstanding example of an ill-conceived, badly executed, and thoroughly detrimental experiment."[5]

In another disaster, in 1959, ten thousand acres of sageland in Wyoming were sprayed with weed killers by the U.S. Forest Service. The purpose was to get rid of the sagebrush and establish grasslands. The sagebrush disappeared all right, but in one very beautiful area so did the willows, and so did the moose that lived among the willows. So did all the beavers and the trout and the waterfowl. All that was left were gray, dying willows and a "tiny creek . . . threading its ways through a bare, hot land where no shade remained."[6]

There were other, similar tales—hundreds—some great, some small, all horrible.

But Carson did not want the book to be only a collection of horror stories. They would be dismissed by authorities who would say, "You really don't have to worry. Yes, there were some mistakes in the past, but nowadays we are much more careful."

She wanted to educate people so that they understood clearly what was going on. She wanted to present her case in detail and with hard scientific facts. To do this, she had to teach the chemistry of DDT and its cousins, how they acted against life, why they were dangerous. She had to show that even when insecticides did not kill, they could severely damage living things, for they attacked life at the level of its cells. She had to prove that even small amounts of pesticides could gradually accumulate and concentrate and persist for many years, poisoning the environment. She had to show that people knew next to nothing about the long-term effects of the billions of gallons of poison being spread over the earth, and that the little they did know was very disquieting. She had to show, almost as in a geometry proof, that the rain of poison onto the natural world did not even kill off the insect pests, but instead produced "super-insects" immune to the poison.

Once people knew the scientific facts, she believed, they would know what actions to take and would not be misled by those who had a financial interest in pesticides.

Throughout 1959, she continued to do research and work on the manuscript. She wrote hopefully to the publisher that she might be finished with it by fall, so that a publication date of February 1960 might be possible. But now she began to have health problems. She was plagued with sinus troubles, and worse things were to follow. The promised dates came and passed, and she wrote, "I guess all that sustains me is a serene inner conviction that when, at last, the book is done, it is going to be built on an unshakable foundation. . . . I am very happy deep down inside with what I have been able to dig out and fit together, but I'm also horribly frustrated that it is taking so long."[7]

Then, in the spring of 1960, she learned that she had a breast tumor. The doctor who operated said that the growth was benign, not malignant. Next she developed an ulcer. She complained wryly that there seemed to be a conspiracy to prevent her from writing the book, but she continued gamely with the work.

As if she were not busy enough, she agreed to do a revision of *The Sea Around Us*, which needed to be updated after ten years, and she served on the committee that wrote up recommendations for the Democratic Party's positions on environmental issues.

But at the end of the year, she learned shocking news: her tumor had not been benign. It was malignant, and it had spread.

Suddenly her life was no longer open and unlimited. It had narrowed to a few years at best. She reacted to the news with calm and courage. She would take radiation treatments for the cancer. The treatments would take a physical and emotional toll on her. "But in the intervals," she wrote in a letter, "I hope to work hard and productively. Perhaps even more than ever, I am eager to get the book done."[8]

Now illness became an important factor in the writing of the book. Carson was bedridden with a bacterial infection early in 1961 and saw the dawning of spring from her bed. But, in spite of her condition, the book was slowly taking shape. In early June she sent in the all-important third chapter, "Deadly Elixirs," which explained the chemistry of pesticides. Other chapters followed slowly. Always Carson had to struggle to keep things simple and clear, and above all accurate. Months passed. Some days were good, her health did not interfere, and the pages flew by. Other days were painful, and little work got done. Sometimes she sat at her desk and wrote; other times she wrote in bed or in a wheelchair. Writing, rewriting, checking and rechecking facts, she slowly brought the book into being. By December 1961, the end was in sight.

Four long years of intense work, far more intense than the work spent on any of her other books, were almost over. Now Carson was haunted by the anxious question of any writer: Would the book work? Would it cut through the public's indifference? Would it wake people up to the peril? Or would it be taken as just another of those dull do-gooder books that made people nod in agreement, and then in boredom? She was sure of her facts. But she could not gauge her poetry. She knew her science, but readers' reactions were out of her hands.

She wrote to a friend in January 1962, ". . . it is a busy time, with now the added spice of excitement with the knowledge that I have almost reached the end of the long road. I'm on the final chapter, but the rest of the [manuscript] is now in the hands of Marie, Paul, Mr. Shawn (*New Yorker*) and the artists. Last night Mr. Shawn telephoned to tell me he had finished reading. His reactions were everything I could have asked or hoped for . . ."[9]

When Carson heard her editor's enthusiastic reaction, she knew that her book would succeed. Shawn had understood her message perfectly; Carson knew that others would, as well.

She was so pleased she picked up her violin and played a Beethoven concerto for her cat, Jeffie. The music released all the emotion that had been building up inside her. She wrote that "the tension of four years was broken and I let the tears come. . . . And . . . the thoughts of all the birds and other creatures and all the loveliness that is in nature came to me with such a surge of deep happiness, that now I had done what I could—I had been able to complete it—now it had its own life."[10]

8

Noisy Summer

Silent Spring started out with a fable. After that it was solid fact all the way. Sometimes it was grim reading. Passages of explanation were followed by amazing stories of human folly and destructiveness. Horrified readers half dreaded to turn the page but were compelled to keep reading.

The book described the growth of the chemical industry, which was really a child of World War II. During that war, in the race to find compounds that killed people, chemicals that killed insects and plants were developed. New chemicals were being introduced into the environment at the rate of five hundred a year, and no one had any idea how they fit into—or broke apart—the web of life. Among those chemicals were the widely used and profitable pesticides. "It is not my contention," Carson wrote, "that chemical insecticides must never be used. I do contend that we have put poisonous and biologically potent chemicals indiscriminately into the hands of persons largely or wholly ignorant of their potentials for harm."[1]

She explained the chemistry of DDT and its cousins and another group of pesticides, the organic phosphates, which were related to nerve gas. These powerful general poisons did not become less dangerous simply because they were familiar to people. After telling some chilling stories of what happened to people who misused the poisons, Carson turned to an examination of their effects in the natural world.

Her first worry was their effect on the waters and streams of the country. Pesticides do not stay where they are sprayed; they run off and are carried away by the rain. They end up polluting rivers, streams, and even water deep in the earth. Carson told of their devastating effects on fish and on other animals that eat the fish. Later in the book, she returned to the plight of the fish, detailing many cases where pesticides had virtually wiped out fish from streams and rivers.

Pesticides in water were, Carson thought, part of a larger problem: America's habit of using its waterways as a dumping place for inconvenient chemicals and wastes. She did not see how the vital waterways could continue to be sources of drinkable water and poison dumps at the same time.

Carson protested the use of waterways as chemical dumps.

And then there was the matter of the soil. What happened to the soil when it was sprayed with pesticides? Soil supports a very complicated community of life, ranging from bacteria to earthworms. Was it reasonable to think that a general poison affected only a single insect or weed? Pesticides could last for years in the soil, and could accumulate through repeated applications. Crops grown in such soil could take up the poisons through their roots, making the food unfit to eat.

Rachel Carson considered weed killers "our latest chemical toy." She maintained that they were carelessly used, both by government agencies to kill unwanted vegetation on millions of acres and by homeowners to control crab grass in their lawns. Again, she related many stories of the misuse of these dangerous poisons and the tragic consequences that followed.

The "war" against various insects had led to many follies. Carson told about the slaughter of birds, squirrels, and even dogs and cats, in the war against the Japanese beetle, when aldrin was sprayed across southeastern Michigan. She told of the annihilation of all the birds and much of the wildlife in a six-year war against the beetle in Illinois. In neither case was the Japanese beetle destroyed. She wrote: "Incidents like the eastern Illinois spraying raise a question that is not only scientific but moral. The question is whether any civilization can wage relentless war on life without destroying itself, and without losing the right to call itself civilized."[2]

Another war, this one against Dutch elm disease, had brought a rain of death upon many species of birds— without, however, stopping the spread of the disease. Again, Carson gave example after example. Aerial wars against gypsy moths and fire ants had the same depressing results but were even more indiscriminate, for airplanes had little control over where their poisonous clouds landed.

Finally, Carson talked about the human costs. She pointed out that government agencies often gave the appearance of protecting health and the environment while in fact aiding the pesticide companies. Citizens who thought that "someone in authority" was looking out for them were naïve.

People seldom keeled over dead after contact with a pesticide. But no one knew what long-term, low-level, sustained exposure to pesticides did to people's health. It seemed impossible to Carson that people would escape scot free from all the effects of poisons that killed insects, plants, fish, birds, and other mammals. No one knew how much pesticide the human body could store up, or what the poisons could do to the body. Doctors suspected that at least some health complaints were caused by the poisons, because they recurred when people were exposed to those poisons again.

Some insecticides had been shown to interfere with the energy-making processes of cells, and some were suspected of causing damaging mutations, or changes in the cell structure. Carson presented evidence that the chemicals so blithely spread about in the environment might well be carcinogenic—cancer-causing—and declared that since they were synthetic, they could and should be eliminated by society.

There was a savage irony in the relentless chemical war on insects. The insects always came back, stronger than before. A billion mosquitoes or houseflies might die from DDT, but the hundreds that survived and bred were immune to DDT, and so were their offspring. If heptachlor was tried next, the same thing happened. And so the cycle went, more powerful chemicals producing more powerful insects until people ran out of new chemicals and the insects won. Meanwhile, useful insects were killed off, or the web of life was so rearranged that formerly unnoticed insects bred wildly out of control and became new pests. So all the pesticide spraying, and all the dead birds and dead animals, were for nothing.

Despite the dire warnings, Carson ended her book on a hopeful note. She admitted that it was necessary to control insects, and said that there had been some careful uses of pesticides that had been notably successful. But there were better ways, which were called "biological controls." In one experiment, huge numbers of sterilized screw flies were released during mating season on the island of Curaçao. The population of this pest fell sharply. Within a year, they were extinct. The release of sterilized insects to control populations of pests seemed an exciting and promising alternative to pesticides. Another biological control was the use of chemical "attractants" to capture and kill insects. And still another approach was to help insect-eating birds, spiders, and mammals to make homes in the insects' environment.

But, Carson wrote, "The current vogue for poisons has failed utterly to take into account these most fundamental considerations. As crude a weapon as the caveman's club, the chemical barrage has been hurled against the fabric of life—a fabric on the one hand delicate and destructible, on the other miraculously tough and resilient, and capable of striking back in unexpected ways."[3]

The first of the three excerpts from *Silent Spring* was printed in *The New Yorker* on June 16, 1962. The reaction was explosive. It could not have been otherwise. Carson had described so many instances of needless death that the wanton destruction of life could not be denied. She had calmly contrasted the ugliness, meanness, and failures of the war against pests with the beauty of the earth that it was destroying. People read, understood, and reacted. They put down the book, picked up a pen, and wrote outraged letters to the editor, to their congressperson, to the mayor, to the government agencies, to anyone in authority, expressing the anger and betrayal they felt.

When the book was published in September, it was an immediate best-seller. It was at the top of the list by October. Carson was accustomed to having best-sellers by now, but this book was different. The incredible sales of *Silent Spring* were proof that she had succeeded in waking people up to the danger.

As Carson had foreseen, she made instant enemies. The chemical manufacturers came out against her book, and so did the food processing industry, agribusinesses, and government agencies from the federal down through the state and county levels that were linked to the agricultural community. Publications, trade associations, and some scientists reacted unfavorably to the book.

Even before the book was published, one chemical company had tried to stop it from coming out. A company official wrote to the publisher, Houghton Mifflin, and complained about inaccuracies in the book. He then suggested that Carson was swayed by "sinister influences" whose mission was "to reduce the use of agricultural chemicals in this country and in the countries of western Europe, so that our supply of food will be reduced to east-curtain parity."[4] By this he meant that these "influences" were trying to bring American food supplies down to the level of those in Eastern Europe. In other words, his suggestion was that Communists in the United States had convinced Carson to write her book, so that chemical production would stop and the United States would cease to be "great."

Many of the scientists who argued with the facts in *Silent Spring* were on the payrolls of chemical companies, or had received grants from those companies, so their statements were suspect. Others, however, honestly felt that the good that was accomplished by spraying pesticides outweighed the harm they did. "What's a few meadowlarks?" one scientist asked.

This was the attitude Carson meant to change. It was clear that the companies were making tremendous profits, and that had to be a reason for their position. What shocked Carson was the fact that they cared so little about the unprecedented environmental problems they had created. They tried to reduce the whole issue to a question of money. While some wildlife might die, the chemical manufacturers argued, agricultural production would soar. They would make good profits, and so it was all worth it.

Carson knew that they could not attack the facts in her book directly. She had done the research, and the facts were on her side. (*New York Times* science reporter Walter Sullivan wrote, "Despite their distress over *Silent Spring,* the [chemical] industry men conceded that most of her facts were correct.")[5] They would have to get at her in other ways. In a speech to the Women's National Press Club in December, Carson dryly analyzed these attacks:

> One obvious way to try to weaken a cause is to discredit the person who champions it. So—the masters of invective and insinuation have been busy: I am a "bird lover—a cat lover—a fish lover," a priestess of nature, a devotee of a mystical cult having to do with laws of the universe which my critics consider themselves immune to. Another well-known, and much used, device is to misrepresent my position and attack the things I have never said . . . Another piece in the pattern of attack largely ignores *Silent Spring* and concentrates on what I suppose would be called the soft sell—the soothing reassurances to the public.[6]

But Carson also had a good many friends and allies. The majority of press and public opinion was on her side. So were much of the scientific community and several newly-formed groups of people who called themselves "environmentalists." Typical of the adulations were these:

> *Silent Spring* is a devastating attack on human carelessness, greed and irresponsibility. It should be read by every American who does not want it to be the epitaph of a world not very far beyond us in time.[7]
>
> *Saturday Review*

Miss Carson does not argue that chemical insecticides must never be used, but she warns of the dangers of misuse and overuse by a public that has become mesmerized by the notion that chemists are the possessors of divine wisdom and that nothing but benefit can emerge from their test tubes.[8]

The *New York Times*

The most important chronicle of this century for the human race.[9]

Supreme Court Justice
William O. Douglas

In addition, prominent naturalists spoke out on Carson's behalf. Loren Eisely, the distinguished anthropologist and writer, and Robert Rudd, a respected entomologist (insect specialist), wrote reviews praising the book.

Carson serenely waited out the controversy. She had no doubts about herself, and she had no doubts about the truthfulness of her book. It was only a matter of time before the truth prevailed.

President Kennedy first read the selections from *Silent Spring* that were published in *The New Yorker*. When the book came out, Jacqueline Kennedy invited Carson to the White House to talk about the use of pesticides. Like most Americans, the Kennedys were concerned about the problem. Unlike most other people, however, the Kennedys had power to act. The president ordered his Science Advisory Committee to explore the matter. Their report, published in May 1963, was the key factor in turning the tide of battle in favor of Rachel Carson and her book. It acknowledged the benefits of chemical pesticides (which Rachel Carson had never questioned), but it condemned the overuse and careless application of pesticides. It also acknowledged the accuracy of Carson's scientific research and endorsed her position.

Science magazine, which had given a hostile review to *Silent Spring*, wrote that "though [the report] is a temperate document, even in tone, and carefully balanced in its assessment of risks versus benefits, it adds up to a fairly thorough-going vindication of Rachel Carson's *Silent Spring* thesis."[10]

A few weeks later, Carson was invited to Senate hearings chaired by Senator Abraham Ribicoff of Connecticut. Ribicoff had read *Silent Spring* and became convinced that it was time that Congress looked into the pesticide problem. Carson appeared before Ribicoff's subcommittee and testified that since environmental issues often became tangled in disputes between government agencies it was necessary to create "an independent board . . . at the level of the Executive Offices" to resolve them.[11]

Several environmental bills were already being considered in Congress. They were the beginning of a great groundswell of environmental legislation. Between 1962 and 1980, a dozen federal laws and hundreds of state laws were passed to protect, regulate, and clean up many different parts of the environment. In 1970, the Environmental Protection Agency was created. It was an independent agency that was part of the Executive Branch, just as Carson had recommended. Two years

Rachel Carson appeared at Senate hearings on pesticides in 1963.

later, working hand in hand with environmental groups, the EPA severely restricted the sale and use of DDT in this country.

Perhaps the most telling sign of the change that Rachel Carson's work had brought about came at the end of the hearings. Senator Ribicoff walked up to Carson when she was finished testifying and held out a book. It was his own copy of *Silent Spring*. He wanted the author to autograph it.

The year 1963 was one of paradox for Rachel Carson. She had fulfilled her highest wish, and her triumph was international. The world rushed to honor her and what she had done. She received countless awards for the book. Perhaps most meaningful to her was the Albert Schweitzer Medal, because Dr. Schweitzer's phrase, "reverence for life" was her own credo, the words she lived by. In one week in December, she was awarded the National Audubon Society Medal and the medal of the American Geographical Society, and was elected as one of the fifty members of the exclusive American Academy of Arts and Letters. The *New York Times* declared in an editorial that she should receive a Nobel Prize.

At the same time, the cancer was spreading and ravaging her body. That spring she had suffered a heart attack. The radiation treatments for the cancer were exhausting her energies. Now she was often confined to a wheelchair or forced to lie in bed. "I keep thinking," she wrote, "if only I could have reached this point ten years ago! Now, when there is an opportunity to do so much, my body falters and I know there is little time left."

Her illness continued and she grew steadily weaker. The high point of her career had come not a moment too soon. Rachel Carson died on April 14, 1964, in Silver Spring, Maryland, at the age of 56. The world mourned her death.

9

Choices

Silent Spring showed that people are not masters of nature, but rather part of nature. It was a revolutionary thought at the time. Today no one seriously questions its truth, but in 1962 it was a direct attack on the values and assumptions of society.

Thomas Kuhn, a historian of science, describes something called a "paradigm shift"—a change in basic assumptions, so that you look at the world from a different angle. The world is still the same, but it looks completely different when seen from the new point of view. Things that once were logical now seem absurd; things that once were unimportant become vital.

There are many examples of paradigm shifts in the history of science. One came in the nineteenth century with Robert Koch's discovery that bacterial germs cause certain types of disease. Before Koch's discovery, people attributed outbreaks of disease to evil spirits, negative thinking, and many other causes. After Koch's germ theory, however, hygiene, vaccines, and other ways of controlling bacteria became important. A major shift in thinking had occurred.

Silent Spring caused just such a paradigm shift. It crystallized the environmental ethic: People are not masters of nature; they are part of nature. The book's publication gave birth to the modern environmental movement in the United States and around the world.

There were long-standing environmental groups, such as the National Audubon Society and the Sierra Club, but these groups had looked upon nature more as a wonderful theater to view than as a fragile whole that humans were capable of upsetting. Now these groups found that new members were joining who were younger, energetic, and devoted to political action.

Also, dozens of new environmental organizations sprang up. In 1967, the Environmental Defense Fund was organized to "build a body of case law to establish citizens' rights to a clean environment." Friends of the Earth, which was started in 1969, soon became an international organization fighting for responsible energy development, sustainable agriculture, and protection of forests.

Then, in 1970, the Environmental Protection Agency (EPA) was formed. It was a small, understaffed government organization at first, but it grew rapidly into the largest environmental agency in the world. And there was no doubt that it was Rachel Carson's call for an "independent board" in the government that brought the EPA into existence. An article in the *EPA Journal* referred to the organization as "the extended shadow of Rachel Carson."

Many critics charge that the EPA has lost sight of Rachel Carson's ideals. The EPA has the daunting task of overseeing the environmental impact of farms, factories, oil and gas companies, auto makers, and waste disposal plants. Perhaps this is too great a task for one group.

Fortunately, the EPA is not alone. In addition to those listed above, dozens of other groups have sprung up across the country and around the world. Some, such as Greenpeace, take a radical stand. Members of Green-

Members of Greenpeace protesting the dumping of chemical waste.

peace literally put their lives on the line to demonstrate the devastation of wildlife. They have put themselves between whaling boats and endangered whales and have led television crews to illegal ocean dumping sites.

Ad hoc groups—groups organized for one specific purpose—have opposed the building of nuclear power plants, the dumping of toxic wastes into rivers, and the systematic poisoning of coyotes in the West or wolves in Alaska.

All of these groups profoundly mistrust the idea of progress through new technology. They take *Silent Spring* as their bible. Rachel Carson had described one environmental issue with such clarity and precision that they could use it as a model for other issues. They knew the forces arrayed against them and the tactics that would be used. Their own battles were extensions of the one that she had fought. The campaigns to save wolves or whales or eagles, the opposition to nuclear power plants, the drive to force automakers to produce fuel-efficient cars, the battle against acid rain and deforestation, the movement to clean up toxic dump sites, and a hundred others were all really one battle—Rachel Carson's battle to force humanity to respect and protect the web of life of which it is a part.

When a new paradigm arises, the old one does not suddenly evaporate. American technology and much of the American lifestyle is still based on the old assumptions that people can exploit the earth and pay no price. Sometimes the environmental ethic becomes a facade behind which the old assumptions continue on. People may go to the park on Earth Day, listen to the earnest speeches, buy books about the environment, and shake their heads when they read about the latest oil spill or leak of radioactivity. But that may be the end of their actions.

People may say, "Of course we must respect our place in nature." But often they do not adjust their lives to reflect this understanding. They continue to use electricity wastefully, to use plastic trash bags when paper ones would do, to buy weed killers for their lawns that will damage the environment. Behind the facade of environmental awareness, the old ways of living continue. Rachel Carson was well aware that action, hard political action, was necessary to bring real change.

As the environmental movement grew, so did awareness of just how serious the problems are. Rachel Carson would not have been surprised. She knew that the devastation caused by pesticides was only one part of a widespread global devastation. She had pointed out that the release of radioactive materials into the environment was a problem in many ways more serious than that of insecticides. But even she would probably be amazed at the scale of the problems uncovered, catastrophes that dwarf anything she described. Here are a half dozen. The list could easily be extended to several dozen.

- Millions of gallons and thousands of tons of radioactive wastes have accumulated at nuclear reactor sites. There is no place to store them for the many centuries they will remain dangerous.

- In the tropics, rain forests are being cut down so rapidly that an area the size of West Virginia is destroyed every year. The rain forests contain half of all species of plants, animals, and insects on the planet. Scientists compare this loss of life to the mass extinctions that ended the age of the dinosaurs. There are many reasons for this destruction, but all are connected to industrial "progress."

- Chemicals called chlorofluorocarbons, or CFCs, used in refrigerators, air conditioners, and aerosol sprays, are destroying ozone in the upper atmosphere. That ozone protects humans from cancer-causing radiation from the sun. The manufacture of CFCs is diminishing, but they will continue to destroy ozone for decades to come.

- Acid rain, created by burning coal, oil, and other factory emissions, has destroyed forests and polluted lakes in large sections of the United States and in many nations around the world.

Factory emissions were unchecked before Silent Spring.

- Many cities and states have run out of places to dump the garbage from homes and factories. The United States once had about six thousand landfills where garbage was dumped. By 1993, about five thousand of them will be full and will have to be closed down. The vast majority of solid waste can be recycled, but efforts have been half-hearted at best. Americans only recycle about ten percent of the garbage they create. The industrialized world is wasting precious natural resources and running out of room to put the waste.

- Industrialized nations burn so much fossil fuel and spew so much carbon dioxide into the atmosphere that we are warming up the entire planet. Scientists concerned about the so-called greenhouse effect believe that in the next hundred years the average temperature of the earth will rise by between four and eight degrees. The effects upon life are unpredictable but are sure to be major and in some cases catastrophic. Some scientists speculate about the possibility of the polar ice caps melting, which would in turn cause flooding of coastal areas, and about plants dying because of the increased temperatures.

Silent Spring did not solve the many environmental problems we have created. It did not even solve the problem of pesticides. But what it did do was awaken in people the recognition that the industrialized world has been on a suicidal course. Now people are awake—sometimes. And they look around in horror and in regret—

sometimes. And they take action—sometimes. Will enough be done in time?

After the publication of *Silent Spring*, Rachel Carson appeared on a television program and defended what she had written. She summarized her beliefs in her usual way: simply, clearly, and with feeling.

"Now, I truly believe that we in this generation must come to terms with nature, and I think we're challenged as mankind has never been challenged before to prove our maturity and our mastery, not of nature, but of ourselves."[1]

That challenge is still with us.

Important Events in Rachel Carson's Life

1907   Born May 27 in Springdale, Pennsylvania.

1918   Writes story for *St. Nicholas* magazine at age 10.

1925   Graduates from Parnassus High School.

1925-29   Attends Pennsylvania College for Women.

1932   Obtains Masters Degree in marine biology.

1936   Becomes junior aquatic biologist at the U.S. Bureau of Fisheries.

1941   *Under the Sea Wind*, her first book, is published.

1946-47   Writes *Conservation in Action* booklets.

1951   *The Sea Around Us* is published.

1955   *The Edge of the Sea* is published.

1958   Receives letter from Olga Huckins about DDT spraying in Massachusetts.

               Carson's mother, Maria, dies in December.

1960   Learns that she has breast cancer.

1962   The first installment of *Silent Spring* appears in *The New Yorker* on June 16.

               Silent Spring is published in September.

1963   Appears before a Senate subcommittee studying "Activities Relating to the use of Pesticides" on June 4.

1964   Dies in Silver Spring, Maryland, on April 14.

1967   The Environmental Protection Agency, called "the extended shadow of Rachel Carson," is established.

Notes

Chapter 1

1. Edwin Diamond, "The Myth of the 'Pesticide Menace,'" *Saturday Evening Post,* September 1962.

2. "Pesticides: The Price for Progress," *Time,* September 28, 1962.

3. Rachel Carson, *Silent Spring* (New York: Fawcett Crest, 1964), p. 18.

4. Carson, *Silent Spring,* p. 13.

5. Carson, *Silent Spring,* p. 14.

6. Frank Graham, Jr., *Since Silent Spring* (Boston: Houghton Mifflin, 1970), p. 56.

7. Graham, p. 51.

8. Paul Brooks, *The House of Life: Rachel Carson* at Work (Boston: Houghton Mifflin, 1972), p. 305.

Chapter 2

1. James M. McPherson, *Battle Cry of Freedom* (New York: Oxford University Press, 1988), p. 90.

2. Brooks, p. 16.

3. Brooks, p. 16.

Chapter 3

1. William A. DeGregorio, *The Complete Book of U.S. Presidents* (New York: Dembner Books, 1984).

2. Sterling, p. 43.

3. Brooks, p. 18.

Chapter 4

1. *The Oxford Book of Twentieth Century English Verse* (Oxford: Clarendon Press, 1973), p. 1590.

2. Brooks, p. 1.

3. Rachel Carson, *The Edge of the Sea* (Boston: Houghton Mifflin, 1955), pp. 168-70.

Chapter 5

1. Brooks, p. 64.

2. Sterling, p. 109.

3. Sterling, p. 111.

4. Brooks, p. 77.

5. Brooks, p. 124.

6. Rachel Carson Council, "The 25th Anniversary of the Publication of *Silent Spring,*" September 27, 1987.

7. Rachel Carson, *The Sea Around Us* (New York: Oxford University Press, 1951). p. 109.

Chapter 6

1. Brooks, p. 131.

2. Brooks, p. 131.

3. Brooks, p. 153.

4. Brooks, p. 158.

5. Rachel Carson, *The Edge of the Sea* (Boston: Houghton Mifflin, 1955), p. 209.

Chapter 7

1. Olga Owens Huckins, letter to the *Boston Herald,* January 29, 1958.

2. Brooks, p. 233.

3. Brooks, p. 235.

4. Carson, *Silent Spring,* p. 147.

5. Carson, *Silent Spring,* p. 147.

6. Carson, *Silent Spring,* p. 68.

7. Brooks, p. 258.

8. Brooks, p. 265.

9. Brooks, p. 271.

10. Brooks, p. 271-72.

Chapter 8

1. Carson, *Silent Spring,* p. 22.

2. Carson, *Silent Spring,* p. 95.

3. Carson, *Silent Spring,* p. 261.

4. Graham, p. 49.

5. Sterling, p. 172.

6. Brooks, p. 303.

7. *Saturday Review,* September 1962.

8. *New York Times,* July 2, 1962.

9. Rachel Carson Council, September 27, 1987.

10. *Science,* May 24, 1963.

11. Rachel Carson, Statement Before the Senate Committee on Commerce, June 6, 1963.

Chapter 9

1. "CBS Reports," "The Silent Spring of Rachel Carson," March 12, 1963.

Suggested Reading

BOOKS BY RACHEL CARSON

Under the Sea Wind. New York: Simon and Schuster, 1941.

The Sea Around Us. New York: Oxford University Press, 1951.

The Edge of the Sea. Boston: Houghton Mifflin, 1955.

Silent Spring. Boston: Houghton Mifflin, 1962.

The Sense of Wonder. New York: Harper and Row, 1965.

BOOKS ABOUT RACHEL CARSON

Harlan, Judith. *Sounding the Alarm: A Biography of Rachel Carson*. Minneapolis: Dillon Press, 1989.

Sterling, Philip. *Sea and Earth: The Life of Rachel Carson*. New York: Thomas Y. Crowell, 1970.

BOOKS ABOUT THE ENVIRONMENT

Caufield, Catherine. *In the Rainforest*. New York: Knopf, 1985.

Earthworks Group. *50 Simple Things You Can Do to Save the Earth*. Berkeley: Earthworks Press, 1989.

Gutnik, Martin J. *Ecology*. New York: Franklin Watts, 1984.

Law, Kevin J. *The Environmental Protection Agency*. New York: Chelsea House, 1988.

Myers, Norman, ed. *Gaia: An Atlas of Planet Management*. New York: Doubleday, 1984.

Index

Acid rain, 87
Agricultural boom, 8-9
Albatross III, 44
Aldrin, 73
American Academy of Arts and
    Letters, 82
American Geographical Society
    Medal, 82
The Arrow, 26
Atlantic Monthly, 35-36, 37
Attractants, 75

Baltimore Sun, 36, 38
Biological control of insects, 75
Birth defects, and thalidomide, 11
Boston Herald, 59, 60
Briggs, Shirley, 44
Brooks, Paul, 65
Brower, David, 10
Bureau of Fisheries, U.S., 8, 32,
    34-37, 41
Burroughs, John, 10

Cancer, 68-69, 82
Carbon dioxide, 89
Carson, Maria McLean (mother),
    20-21, 23, 26, 39, 66
Carson, Marian (sister), 19, 36
Carson, Rachel
    as best-selling author, 49, 51,
        52-54
    at Bureau of Fisheries, 32, 34-37
    cancer, 68-69, 82
    and *Conservation in Action*,
        42-44
    death of, 82
    early life, 18-22
    and *Edge of the Sea*, 56-57
    education, 21-30
    at Fish and Wildlife Service, 41,
        42, 54-55
    as Information Division
        editor-in-chief, 44

at Johns Hopkins University,
    30, 31, 34
and Mu Sigma, 29
at Pennsylvania College for
    Women, 23-30
prizes and awards, 53, 82
and Saxton fellowship, 48
and *The Sea Around Us*,
    45-50, 68
and spraying of pesticides,
    60-63
studies biology, 27-30
and *Under the Sea Wind*, 37-40,
    50-51
at University of Maryland, 34
and violin, 26
at Woods Hole, 30, 32-34, 44
writing, 21-22, 26-27, 35-37
Carson, Robert (brother), 19, 34
Carson, Robert (father), 18-19, 20,
    23, 34, 36
"CBS Reports," 13
Chincoteague Refuge, 44
Chlorofluorocarbons, 87
Codman, R. C., 60, 61
Conservation in Action, 42-44
Coolidge, Calvin, 25
Coolidge, Cora, 24
Cowles, R. P., 31, 33
Croff, Grace, 29

DDT, 12, 60-61, 63, 67, 75, 81
Diamond, Edwin, 8
Dieldrin, 66
Douglas, William O., 79
Dutch elm disease, 73

Earth Day, 86
Ecology, 56
The Edge of the Sea, 56-57
Eiseley, Loren, 79
Emerson, Ralph Waldo, 42
Englicode, 26-27

Environmental Defense Fund, 84
Environmental Protection Agency
    (EPA), 80-81, 84
EPA Journal, 84

Fire ants, 66, 74
Fish and Wildlife Service, U.S., 8,
    41, 42, 54-55
Fisher, Charlotte, 23
Forest Service, U.S., 67
French, Howard, 39
Friends of the Earth, 84
Frye, Mary, 33

Good Housekeeping, 64
Greenpeace, 84-85
Gypsy moths, 64, 74

Heptachlor, 66
Herbicides. *See* Pesticides
Higgins, Elmer, 34-37
Hines, Bob, 44
Houghton Mifflin, 54, 64, 76
Howe, Quincy, 37, 38
Huckins, Olga, 59, 60-62

Insecticides. *See* Pesticides

Japanese beetle, 73
Johns Hopkins University, 30, 31

Kennedy, Jacqueline, 79
Kennedy, John F., 14-15, 17, 79-80
Koch, Robert, 83
Krumpe, Mildred, 23
Kuhn, Thomas, 83

Leopold, Aldo, 10, 42
Lincoln, Abraham, 17

Marine Biological Laboratory. *See*
    Woods Hole
Masefield, John, 32
Mattamuskeet Refuge, 44
Migratory Bird Conservation
    Act, 42

Mosquitos, and DDT, 60-61
Muir, John, 10, 42
Mu Sigma, 29

National Audubon Society, 84
    Medal, 82
National Book Award, 53
National Park Service, 42
New Yorker, 7, 49, 56, 64, 76
New York Times, 49-50, 79, 82

Oceanographic Institution, 33
Oliver, Edith, 49
Oxford University Press, 47, 49

Paradigm shift, 83
Parnassus High School, New
    Kensington, 23
Pennsylvania College for Women,
    23-30, 53
Pesticides, 9-10, 14, 15, 60-63,
    68-69, 72-75
Phosphates, 71
Pollution and pesticides, 72-73
Potter, Beatrix, 21
President's Science Advisory
    Committee, 15, 80
Prizes and awards, 53, 82

Radioactive wastes, 87
Radio programs, 35
Rain forest destruction, 87
Ribicoff, Abraham, 80, 81
Rockefeller Institution, 33
Rodell, Marie, 47, 49, 54, 63
"A Romance Under the Waters,"
    35
Roosevelt, Theodore, 42
Rudd, Robert, 79

Saint Nicholas, 22
Saturday Evening Post, 7
Saturday Review, 78
Eugene F. Saxton Memorial
    Fellowship, 48
Albert Schweitzer Medal, 82

Science, 80
Scientific Book Club, 40
Screw flies, 75
The Sea Around Us, 8, 45-50, 68
"Sea-Fever" (Masefield), 32
Shawn, William, 49, 70
Sierra Club, 14, 84
Silent Spring, 7-8, 10-14, 69-80
    and paradigm shift, 83-90
Simon and Schuster, 37, 38
Skinker, Mary Scott, 28-30, 31
"Something About the Sky," 59
Stowe, Harriet Beecher, 17
Sullivan, Walter, 77

Tennyson, Alfred, Lord, 27
Thalidomide, 11
Thoreau, Henry David, 10, 42

Uncle Tom's Cabin (Stowe), 17
"Undersea," 37
Under the Sea Wind, 37-40, 50-51
University of Maryland, 34

Van Loon, Hendrik Willem, 37, 38
Vaudrin, Philip, 47, 49

Walden (Thoreau), 10
Washington Female Seminary, 20
Water pollution and pesticides, 72
Weed killers. See Pesticides
White, E. B., 64
Wildlife refuges, 42-43
Women's National Press Club,
    77-78
Woods Hole Marine Biological
    Laboratory, 30, 32-34, 44